The Anglican Prayer Life

The Anglican Prayer Life

'Ceum na Còrach'
The True Way

The Rev. Dr. David F. Sokol

Writers Club Press
San Jose New York Lincoln Shanghai

The Anglican Prayer Life
'Ceum na Còrach' The True Way

All Rights Reserved © 2001 by The Rev. Dr. David F. Sokol

No part of this book may be reproduced or transmitted in any form or by any means, graphic, electronic, or mechanical, including photocopying, recording, taping, or by any information storage retrieval system, without the permission in writing from the publisher.

Writers Club Press
an imprint of iUniverse.com, Inc.

For information address:
iUniverse.com, Inc.
5220 S 16th, Ste. 200
Lincoln, NE 68512
www.iuniverse.com

ISBN: 0-595-19171-1

Printed in the United States of America

To my wonderful bride Patricia, and our beautiful daughter Katherine
who consistently support our family life-in-Christ
and who share a wonderful English sense of humor.

"The Lord was not in the wind…the Lord was not in the earthquake…the Lord was not in the fire…and after the fire, a sound of gentle stillness" (1Kings 19:11-12)

Contents

Preface xi
Acknowledgements xvii
Introduction xix
Part One: Understanding The "Prayer Life" 1
    What Prayer Does 3
    Why We Pray 9
    How to Pray 28
Part Two: Preparation for a Prayer-Filled Experience 53
    The Preparation Process 55
Part Three: Types of Prayer and Their Proper Exercise 71
    Let's Talk About Prayer 73
    Simple Prayer 86
    Prayers of Confession or Supplication 89
    Sacramental or Incarnational Prayer 91
    Prayers of Thanksgiving 96
    Prayers of Adoration, Praise and Oblation 98
    Prayer of Petition 104
    Prayer of Intercession 109
    Prayer of Meditation 117
    Prayer of Contemplation 125
    Unceasing Prayer 133
    Covenantal Prayer 143

Part Four: Prayer Exercises 151
    Preparation for the Exercises 153
    The First Prayer Exercise:
    A Person Beginning Serious Prayer 156
    The Second Prayer Exercise:
    Confession or Lamentation Period 163
    The Third Prayer Exercise:
    The Final Phase of the Process 175

Appendix One Prayer Ministry: Anamchara (Prayer Mate) 185

Appendix Two Prayer Ministry: Prayer Groups 189

Appendix Three Prayer Ministry: A Prayer Retreat 197

About the Author 199

Preface

Welcome to the Anglican prayer life! This text should be beneficial to you as you continue your journey of faith within the Church. The pages that follow may simply instruct as a reference document found helpful from time to time if that is what you desire; or they may inform a broader approach within ongoing parish prayer groups or in more formal 'prayer retreats.'

Let's take a moment to preface the remainder of this text to acquaint us with certain concepts, beliefs and traditions. Once accomplished, the subsequent sections should be more revealing to you, 'anamchara' (prayer mate).

Before we proceed further in our text, it is important to know that the word 'pray' means to speak, or better, to "communicate" (Greek *euchesthai*, Latin *precari*, French *prier*, to plead, to beg, to ask earnestly). It has the same etiology as orator and oral. For Christians, prayer is spiritual communication, an act of the **"virtue" of religion** that consists in *asking proper gifts or graces from God.*

In a more general sense prayer is the application of the mind to divine things, not merely to acquire knowledge of them but to make use of such knowledge as a means of union with God. This can be done by acts of praise and thanksgiving, but *petition is the principal act of prayer.* We will review the nature of differing prayer contents later in your reading.

The words used to express prayer in Scripture are: to call up (Gen., 4:26); to intercede (Job, 22:10); to mediate (Is., 53:10); to consult (I

Kings, 28:6); to beseech (Ex., 32:11); and, very commonly, to cry out to. The Fathers speak of it as the elevation of the mind to God with a view to asking proper things from Him (St. John Damascene, *De fide*, 3, 24, in P.G., XCIV, 1090); communing and conversing with God (St. Gregory of Nyssa, *De oratione dom.*, in P.G., XLIV, 1125); talking with God (St. John Chrysostom, *Homily. xxx* in Gen., n. 5, in P.G., LIII, 280). It is therefore the expression of our desires to God whether for us or for others. This expression is not intended to instruct or direct God on what He should do, but to appeal to His goodness. And the appeal is necessary, not because He does not know of our needs or sentiments, but to give definite form to our concerns, to concentrate our whole attention on what we have to recommend to Him, to help us appreciate our close personal relation with Him—*to give form to our Faith*. The expression need not be external or vocal; internal or mental expression can, with a maturing prayer life, eventually be sufficient.

Though some Protestant faiths limit spiritual communication only with God the Father (at times through Jesus Christ), Anglican tradition is more inclusive. Like the Roman and Orthodox understanding, prayer is appropriate for the entire Communion of Saints in the Church Militant, Church Expectant, and Church Triumphant.

Only God is worthy of our worship (trust), but spiritual communication is the duty of all Christians, living and dead. Petitioning that a saint intercede on our behalf, or charging our earthly friends to pray for us is appropriate because the Church (the saints on earth and the Saints in Heaven) is one family and it is our duty to pray for one another. The Anglican understanding of the comprecation of saints and angels means that we acknowledge our oneness,

> *O Almighty God, who hast knit together thine elect in one communion and fellowship…* The Collect, All Saints Day, BCP 256 (1928),

with all the saints (witnesses) living and dead, and our interdependence on one another for witness, support, and intercession. Comprecation means 'abiding in this fellowship of love and prayer.'

The witnesses who have preceded us into the kingdom, "Wherefore seeing we also are compassed about with so great a cloud of witnesses, let us lay aside every weight, and the sin which doth so easily beset us, and let us run with patience the race that is set before us," (Heb 12:1) especially those whom the Church recognizes as saints, share in the living tradition of prayer by the example of their lives, the transmission of their writings, and their prayer today. They contemplate God and constantly praise him. When they entered into the joy of their Maker, they were put in charge of many things; "His lord said unto him, Well done, thou good and faithful servant: thou hast been faithful over a few things, I will make thee ruler over many things: enter thou into the joy of thy lord." (Matt 25:21) Their intercession is their most exalted service to God's plan. We certainly may ask them to intercede for us and for the whole world.

In the communion of saints, many and varied spiritualities developed throughout the history of the churches. The personal charism of some witnesses to God's love for men has been handed on, like "the spirit" of Elijah to Elisha and John the Baptist, so that their followers may have a share in this spirit. "And it came to pass, when they were gone over, that Elijah said unto Elisha, Ask what I shall do for thee, before I be taken away from thee. And Elisha said, I pray thee, let a double portion of thy spirit be upon me." (2 Ki 2:9) "Forasmuch as many have taken in hand to set forth in order a declaration of those things which are most surely believed among us," (Luke 1:1) A distinct spirituality can also arise at the point of convergence of liturgical and theological currents, bearing witness to the integration of the faith into a particular human environment and its history. The different schools of Christian spirituality share in the living tradition of prayer and are essential guides for the faithful. In their rich diversity they are refractions of the one pure light of the Holy Spirit.

Although there is a difference of opinion between Anglicans concerning the "Communion of the Saints" and, specifically, asking for their intercession, such sterilization of the saints is not called for in Scripture or in the Thirty Nine Articles of the Church of England and their subsequent revisions.

In 1553 Article XXII in part read… "The Romish doctrine concerning…invocation of saints, is a fond thing vainly invented, and grounded upon no warranty of Scripture, but rather repugnant to the word of God." The term "doctrina Romanensium" or Romish doctrine was substituted for the "doctrina scholasticorum" or the doctrine of the school authors in 1563 to bring the condemnation up to date subsequent to the Council of Trent.

As E.J. Bicknell writes, invocation may mean either of two things: the simple request to a saint for his prayers (intercession), 'ora pro nobis,' or a request for some particular benefit. In medieval times the saints had come to be regarded as themselves the authors of blessings. Such a view was condemned but the former was affirmed.

There was some evidence that the distinction between the two kinds of invocation was recognized at the Reformation. They were distinguished in the Bishop's Book and the King's Book. In the first of these books 'invocation' is quite definitely used of such prayer as should be made to God alone, and such invocation is contrasted with requests to the saints for prayers.

> *"To pray to Saints to be intercessors with us and for us to our dear Lord for our suits which we make to Him, and for such things as we can obtain none, but of Him, so that we make no invocations to them, is lawful and allowed by the Catholic Church."*

In the second book the language is changed, but though this technical use of 'invocation' is withdrawn, the distinction between the two kinds is maintained.

The practice of invocation makes the communion of saints a reality. It is the unbroken custom of the Catholic Church in East and West alike since the fourth century.

Again, as Bicknell writes "…individuals are left perfectly free to adopt such invocation in their own private prayers…" Scripture and church tradition are peculiarly silent on this issue as specifically defined.

Thus, our worship tradition is based on a three-part structure. Martin Thornton calls it the Catholic Threefold Rule, and provides a detailed presentation of the Rule in his books. Michael Ramsey, the one hundredth Archbishop of Canterbury, refers to it as the Benedictine triangle. The three elements

- Eucharist,
- Office, and
- Personal devotion,

comprise the fundamentals of a disciplined Christian spirituality in the Anglican tradition.

The use of the Rule is a movement away from a series of devotions and unrelated religious "rules" toward an integrated Rule grounded in the worship and prayer life of the One Holy Catholic and Apostolic Church as expressed in the Book of Common Prayer. The Rule is a system that holds together transcendence and immanence, discipline and freedom, common prayer and personal devotions, objective and subjective, reason and emotion.

Through the Rule the parish joins in the tradition and practice of the larger Church and so approaches and participates in that grace-filled life. The Prayer Book assumes that the individual Christian is engaged in personal forms of devotion as well.

The parish's prayer life needs balance, discipline, and order. It also needs experimentation. The Rule recognizes the uniqueness of each parish and person's spiritual life and the paradox that this uniqueness is finally known only from within the Body of Christ.

Although this little book will not focus on such arguments pro-and-con concerning intercession, it is important to understand the Anglican tradition through the ages. Intercession and variation in personal prayers was and is fully accepted with the exception of belief that a 'saint' can provide/create blessings in response to prayer of his or her own volition. And since this superstition and cultic belief of the middle ages has long-since vanished, there should be no worry on that account.

We have a rich and faithful prayer history within the Anglican tradition with its source in Jesus Christ and developed through the Apostles, the Desert Fathers, the Celtic traditions and all the saints both living and dead. Our traditions encourage individual and corporate prayer styles allowing you to find the best means to speak with our Lord and Saviour, Jesus Christ; whether through your petition or through others by intercession.

May your journey be a wonderful, God-filled experience!

Acknowledgements

For the immutable, unchanging and inspired Word of Scripture
And the innumerable texts of learned expression that
form and reform to the needs of the age and the purpose at hand;
such texts in untold numbers both past and present were of benefit to
this book.

The Rt. Rev. Louis Campese, Bishop Ordinary,
Diocese of the Eastern United States, Anglican Church in America,
A wonderful and Godly Bishop, who serves as a
true mentor, teacher and pastor to his priests and deacons.

Cross and Cover Design by John W. Scott, owner of High Cross
Monument Co., Beaumont, TX 1-800-862-2686,
www.HighCrossMonument.com

And, finally, the parishioners of Christ Anglican Church
Who provide such unselfish example to this priest in their daily lives.

Introduction

At the outset, let us understand that we must wrestle and overcome the giants of laziness, inattention, and worst of all—disregard. By disregard I mean the unawareness, the imperceptions, of the utter necessity of making this practice, 'prayer,' the center of our spiritual life. Many have heard of various styles of prayer and practice, many have enjoyed lectures and books on the subject of prayer and yet have never taken up the practice in earnest. Why? They simply did not make the connection between the beautiful theory and the everyday actions of their own lives. This is pretty much the trouble in all religion—people do not make the connection or transition from the theoretical to the practical. As Leo the Great, Bishop of Rome writes in *Sermon XV, Part IV*, 425AD; "Prayer, fasting and almsgiving are the three comprehensive duties of a Christian." It is essential that the connection to a "practiced" prayer life be made to be fully a Christian.

Given the Jewish heritage of Christians and the Jewish 'earthiness' of Anglicans in particular, we should understand the Jewish Chassidic teaching on prayer (2.1)

> "Prayer is the Jew's main weapon. Whatever battles a person has to fight, whether against his evil inclination, or against those who put barriers and obstacles in his path, they should all be fought with prayer. Prayer is the source of our very life. If you want to attain the true holiness of Israel you must pray

profusely. Speak to God and beg Him to help you in every way. Prayer is the weapon with which to win the battle"

In practice we must transfer our awareness from the busy, worldly mind to the silent contemplation of the spirit, from the outer to the inner, from the many to the One. Since, within Anglicanism in the Jewish tradition, we are operating on three levels of body, mind, and spirit, we must ensure that appropriate transition occurs from the body and mind to the spirit. It is through a disciplined approach that prayer will occur.

Perhaps you have never prayed before except in anguish or terror. It may be that the only time the Divine Name has been on your lips has been in angry expletives. But that is the past...at this moment. Jesus waits for you with open arms.

Perhaps you do not believe in prayer. You may have tried to pray and were completely disappointed. Your faith seems to be weakening or completely dried up as in a desert. But that is the past...at this moment Jesus waits for you with open arms.

Perhaps you bear scars, tears, hurts from the pressures and disillusionments of life. Others do not keep their word. They do not seem to care for you or for others. You seem to have memories that keep surfacing; they keep your emotions in turmoil, even when you try to extinguish them. Because of these things you cannot pray; you are not ready or you are not worthy to approach our Saviour. But that is the past....at this moment Jesus waits for you with open arms.

Perhaps you have prayed for months or years but you are now lost in the forest, stranded in the desert, marooned on an island. You begin to feel that prayer is unimportant, lackluster, broken. Your requests seem to fall on deaf ears. You wonder why nothing has happened although your heart aches for yourself or others. God now seems remote, inaccessible, does not listen to you in your time of need or that of others for whom you pray. Listen! That is in the past...at this moment Jesus waits for you with open arms.

Perhaps you have seen the power of prayer. You know of its goodness and affect. But you desire a closer, more intimate relationship with our Lord. There should be no doubt in your mind....at this moment Jesus waits for you with open arms.

Prayer is a sharing in the divine nature, a taking of manhood into God. An interesting thought of the Eastern mystics, that 'prayer is God.' All depends upon the kind of relationship that we have with God, and the kind of God that we believe in.

In prayer we are seeking to achieve a continuous state of recollection and wakefulness to the reality and presence of God. Prayer then is closely linked with knowledge. It is not a cold, calculating set of facts but what the Greek Fathers called *theoria*...a passionate, contemplative insight, involving communion and sharing. Prayer is closely linked and inseparable from theology. Thus, we emphasize *both* the prayers in the Book of Common Prayer and personal prayers as informed by Scripture.

Although we may experience a triggering moment in prayer, Christian life is more than a series of such moments; it is a life in which God is seen and known through the actual process of living and being. "Blessed are the pure in heart: for they shall see God." (Matt 5:8) The aim and goal of Christian life and prayer is to see God.

E. M. Bounds writes:

"Holiness is wholeness, and so God wants holy men, men whole-hearted and true, for his service and for the work of praying. Soul, spirit and body are to unite in all things pertaining to life and godliness. The body, first of all, engages in prayer, since it assumes the praying attitude in prayer. The attitude of the body counts much in prayer, although it is true that the heart may be haughty and lifted up, and the mind listless and wandering, and the praying a mere form, even while the knees are bent in prayer.

The very first step in prayer is a mental one. The disciples took that first step when they said to Jesus at one time, "Lord, teach us to pray." We must be taught through the intellect, and just in so far as the intellect is given up to God in prayer, will we be able to learn well and readily the lesson of prayer.

Nowhere does it appear so clearly that it requires the entire man in all departments of his being, to pray than in this teaching of Paul. It takes the whole man to pray till all the storms that agitate his soul are calmed to a great calm, till the stormy winds and waves cease as by a godlike spell. *It takes the whole man to pray till cruel tyrants and unjust rulers are changed in their natures and lives, as well as in their governing qualities, or till they cease to rule. It requires the entire man in praying till high and proud and unspiritual ecclesiastics become gentle, lowly and religious, till godliness and gravity bear rule in church and in state, in home and in business, in public as well as in private life.* (This author's emphasis)

Prayer is far-reaching in its influence and in its gracious effects. It is intense and profound business that deals with God and his plans and purposes, and it takes whole-hearted men to do it. No half-hearted, half-brained, half-spirited effort will do for this serious, all-important, heavenly business. It is of the nature of a great battle, a conflict to win, a great battle to be fought...this is a life-and-death struggle for a Christian."

The Complete Works of E.M. Bounds on Prayer, Baker Book House, 1990

To see God requires a renewal of our minds. "And be not conformed to this world: but be ye transformed by the renewing of your mind, that ye may prove what is that good, and acceptable, and perfect, will of God." (Rom 12:2) In prayer we open ourselves out to God... a liberating and awakening experience. God breaks out like light in the morning. "Then shall thy light break forth as the morning, and thine health shall spring forth speedily: and thy righteousness shall go before thee; the glory of the LORD shall be thy reward." (Isa 58:8)

Our human experience of God is often times described as an awakening, a heightening of consciousness and perception. To know God is to know one's true self…the ground of one's being. Prayer may start with the experience of sheer wonder and amazement at the natural world. We may find ourselves filled with awe, and this involves both fear, and reassurance that, deep down, the universe is filled with glory. "Thou hast beset me behind and before, and laid thine hand upon me. Such knowledge is too wonderful for me; it is high, I cannot attain unto it. Whither shall I go from thy spirit? or whither shall I flee from thy presence? If I ascend up into heaven, thou art there: if I make my bed in hell, behold, thou art there. If I take the wings of the morning, and dwell in the uttermost parts of the sea; Even there shall thy hand lead me, and thy right hand shall hold me." (Ps 139:5-10)

"Transparent" is an apt description of the attitude of openness that develops as we let the Word speak to us and let our response to Him represent ourselves and our attitudes more fully, and sometimes we must repeat and repeat and repeat our feelings before we feel the transparent nature take hold…the removal of the blocking feelings and the rejuvenation of our true relationship.

The more experience we have in prayer, the more likely we are to let more than thought enter our prayer. We will find ourselves spontaneously seeking ways of expressing ourselves more fully. The prayer deepens, and as it does, it gradually draws into its dynamic more and more dimensions of our lives. Our social and economic attitudes, our interpersonal relationships, our choice of friends, our choice of work, all begin to be affected by the relationship between ourselves and God as that relationship is expressed in personal prayer.

We find such wonder and acceptance in our heritage of Celtic Prayers.

God with me lying down,
God with me rising up,
God with me in each ray of light,
Nor a ray of joy without Him,
    Nor one ray without Him.

Christ with me sleeping,
Christ with me waking,
Christ with me watching,
Every day and night,
    Each day and night.

God with me protecting,
The Lord with me directing,
The Spirit with me strengthening,
For ever and for evermore,
    Ever and evermore, Amen
    Chief of chiefs, Amen.

The Celtic Vision; Selections from the Carmina Gadelica, St. Bede's Publications, 1988, Editor, Esther de Waal

William Blake described our need to go beyond our known world as well.

Unless the eye catch fire
    The God will not be seen
Unless the ear catch fire
    The God will not be heard.
Unless the tongue catch fire
    The God will not be named

> Unless the heart catch fire
> > The God will not be loved
> Unless the mind catch fire
> > The God will not be known.

Prayer is a part of our salvation. It is a distinct precept of Christ in the Gospels (Matt., 4: 9; 7:7; Luke, 8:9; John, 16:26; Col., 4:2; Rom., 12:12; I Pet., 4:7). Without prayer we cannot resist temptation, or grow and mature in God's Grace. This necessity is important to all regardless of their different states in life, but especially to those who by virtue of their office, of priesthood, for instance, or other special religious obligations (altar guild, women's groups, men's orders, rosary sodalities, etc.), should in a **special manner** pray for their own welfare and for others.

The obligation to pray is incumbent on us at all times, not that prayer should be our sole occupation, as the Euchites, or Messalians, and similar heretical sects professed to believe. The texts of Scripture bidding us to pray without ceasing mean that we must pray whenever it is necessary, as it so frequently is necessary; that we must continue to pray. Some writers speak of a virtuous life as an uninterrupted prayer, and appeal to the adage "to toil is to pray" (*laborare est orare*). This does not mean that virtue or labor replaces the duty of prayer, since it is not possible either to practice virtue or to labor properly without frequent use of prayer. The Wyclifites and Waldenses, according to Suarez, advocated what they called vital prayer, consisting in good works, to the exclusion even of all vocal prayer except the Our Father. For this reason Suarez does not approve of the expression (*laborare est orare*), though St. Francis de Sales uses it to mean prayer reinforced by work, or rather work that is inspired by prayer.

The practice of the Church, devoutly followed by the faithful, is to begin and end the day with prayer using the Offices of the Book of Common Prayer if at all possible. Other forms of prayer may be added (as we will review) but the importance here is that you know, and that you pray!

Prayer then is closely allied with vision and insight. We must approach time in a new way. We need to slow down and look deeply within.

__Let us begin!__

Part One:

Understanding The "Prayer Life"

What Prayer Does

"But when he was yet a great way off, his father saw him, and had compassion, and ran, and fell on his neck, and kissed him."
—Luke 15:20.

What does being "a great way off" mean…certainly not what a casual listener might believe. It is not the position of the man who is careless and entirely regardless of God; for you notice that the prodigal spoken of in this scripture is represented now as having awakened, and as returning to his father's house.

Though it is true that all sinners are a great way off from God, whether they know it or not, yet in this particular instance, the position of the poor prodigal is intended to signify the character of one, who has been aroused by conviction, who has been led to abhor his former life, and who sincerely desires to return to God.

But the question; who is the man, and why is he said to be a great way off? For he seems to be very near the kingdom, now that he knows his need and is seeking the Saviour.

In the first place, he is a great way off in his own fears. You read this passage and you have an idea that never was man so far from God as you are. You look back upon your past life, and you recollect how you have slighted God, neglected his Scripture, and rejected all the invitations of his mercy. You turn over the pages of your history, and you remember the sins which you have committed—the sins of your youth and your former transgressions, the crimes of your adulthood, and the sins of your older years; like black waves crashing upon a dark shore, they roll in wave upon wave. There comes a little wave of your childish mistakes, and over that there leaps one of your youthful transgressions, and over the head of this there comes a storm surge of your adulthood transgressions. At the sight of them you stand astonished and amazed

When the light of God's grace comes into your heart, it is something like the opening of the windows of an old cellar that has been closed for a very long time. Down in that cellar, which has not been opened for many months, even years, are all kinds of creatures scurrying about. The walls are dark and damp; it is a place in which no one would willingly enter. You may walk there in the dark very securely, and except now and then for the touch of some slimy creature living in your cellar, you would not believe the place was so bad. Open those shutters, clean a pane of glass through true prayer, let a little light in, and now you see how a thousand undesirable, putrid things have made this place their home. It was not the light that made this place so horrible, but it was the light that showed how horrible it was before. Just open a window, begin your prayer life, and let the light into your soul, and you will be amazed to see at what a distance you are from God.

But back to the Prodigal! At last, from the summit of a mountain, he views his father's house far away in the plain. There are many miles between him and his father whom he has neglected. Can you feel his emotions when, for the first time after so long an absence, he sees the old house at home? He remembers it well in the distance, for though it is a long time since he walked its floors he has never ceased to remember it; and the remembrance of his father's kindness, and of his own prosperity when he was with him, has never been erased from his mind. You would imagine that for one moment he feels a flash of joy, like some flash of lightning in the midst of a Florida storm, but no, darkness comes over his spirit. He will think, "Oh! Suppose I could reach my home, will my father receive me? Won't he shut the door in my face and tell me to go away and spend the rest of my life where I spent the first of it?" Then another thought: "Or maybe, I may even die upon the road, and so, before I have received my father's blessing, my soul may stand before God."

I believe that each of these thoughts has crossed your mind if you are now in the position of one who is seeking Christ, and exist as worries because you are far away from him. It is important that you struggle with these issues. *Before your prayer life becomes real, becomes a part of your Faith, you must avail yourself of confession and the prayer of reconciliation through your parish priest either individually or through a true corporate confession prior to the reception of the Holy Eucharist.* As our contemporary brethren say, "you must be right with the Lord," before you may benefit from intimacy with him; *the intimacy of prayer.*

Christian healing is not a televangelist practicing staged "faith healing." The threefold restoration of broken relationships we call by the theological name of 'reconciliation.' It is the most radical form of healing. In a sense, every form of reconciliation is a healing, and every healing is a form of reconciliation. The two are inseparably linked together in the mission of Christ and his Church. Just as reconciliation radically restores your relationship with God, your neighbor and yourselves, so healing gives us the means to live this restored relationship in our daily lives. Healing is as essential to the Christian life as is necessary for human life. Christians need both reconciliation and healing. Remove one or the other and there is no living God left. Christians everywhere accept the word 'reconciliation,' but many find it difficult to appreciate the true meaning of 'healing.' It will help to clarify the issue if we describe what we mean by both words.

"And all things are of God, who hath reconciled us to himself by Jesus Christ, and hath given to us the ministry of reconciliation" (2 Cor 5:18). Reconciliation is the new life of the Spirit by which we are introduced into a new loving relationship with God our Father, from which flow true loving relationships with our neighbor, and a true love of ourselves through the power of the Spirit of Christ.

The prayer of reconciliation gives us a new heart; healing pumps the blood to every part of our body. Jesus came to save us as total beings of his creation. The Hebrews, among whom he ministered in his earthly life, did not think of a person as divided into mind, body and soul, but as a whole person inclusive of body, soul, feelings and a personal historical background stretching back in the human family tree. For the Hebrews, to heal a person was to heal him in all ways.

Soul: He heals by forgiving us our sins, so enabling us to allow that forgiveness to flow out to others, and not least of all to ourselves.

Emotions: He heals by mending hurtful memories or anxiety caused by stress, irrational guilt, fear and all those psychological upsets that disturb our peace of mind and soul.

Body: He heals illnesses caused by physical diseases or defects that hinder us from the loving service of God our Father and our neighbor.

Healing flows from prayer and gives it authenticity. Jesus believed that when, in faith and trust, he prayed to his Father his requests were granted. "Ask, and it shall be given you; seek, and ye shall find; knock, and it shall be opened unto you: For every one that asketh receiveth; and he that seeketh findeth; and to him that knocketh it shall be opened." (Matt 7:7-8) The promise is there for all his followers, limited only by their faith. The tragedy is that our prayer, like our faith, is too shallow and selfish. "Verily, verily, I say unto you, He that believeth on me, the works that I do shall he do also; and greater works than these shall he do; because I go unto my Father. And whatsoever ye shall ask in my name, that will I do, that the Father may be glorified in the Son. If ye shall ask any thing in my name, I will do it." (John 14:12-14) In the very asking, we find healing.

"Prayer is, then, to speak more boldly, 'converse with Jesus Christ.' Though whispering, consequently, and not opening the lips, we speak in silence, yet we cry inwardly." (John 14:12-14) As we read an important scriptural citation in Clement of Alexandria, *The Stromata or Miscellanies, Book VII, Chapter VII*, AD217

"Now Hannah, she spake in her heart; only her lips moved, but her voice was not heard: therefore Eli thought she had been drunken. And Eli said unto her, How long wilt thou be drunken? put away thy wine from thee. And Hannah answered and said, No, my lord, I am a woman of a sorrowful spirit: I have drunk neither wine nor strong drink, but have poured out my soul before the LORD."

(1 Sam 1:13-15)

But if any occasion of converse with God becomes prayer, no opportunity of access to God ought to be omitted

As we read in *Letter II; Basil to Gregory*, St. Basil, AD364: "Prayers, too, after reading, find the soul fresher, and more vigorously stirred by love towards God. And that prayer is good which imprints a clear idea of God in the soul; and having God established in self by means of memory is, God's indwelling. Thus we become God's temple, when the continuity of our recollection is not severed by earthly cares; when the mind is harassed by no sudden sensations; when the worshipper flees from all things and retreats to God, drawing away all the feelings that invite him to self-indulgence, and passes his time in the pursuits that lead to virtue."

Prayer is the wall of faith: her arms protect us against the foe that keeps watch on us on all sides. So, never walk 'unarmed.' Under the arms of prayer we guard the standard of our King; we await in prayer the angel's trumpet. "In a moment, in the twinkling of an eye, at the last trump: for the trumpet shall sound, and the dead shall be raised incorruptible, and we shall be changed." (1 Cor 15:52) What more then, touching the office of prayer? Even the Lord Himself prayed; to whom be honor and virtue unto the ages of the ages?

Likewise prayer: "…washes away faults, repels temptations, extinguishes persecutions, consoles the faint-spirited, cheers the high-spirited, escorts travelers, appeases waves, makes robbers stand aghast, nourishes the poor, governs the rich, upraises the fallen, arrests the failing, confirms the standing." (Tertullian: Part Third—*Ethical, Book III, On Prayer*, Chapter 29 AD220)

"Again I say unto you, That if two of you shall agree on earth as touching any thing that they shall ask, it shall be done for them of my Father which is in heaven. For where two or three are gathered together in my name, there am I in the midst of them." (Matt 18:19-20)

These are almost frightening words! They reveal to us the most attractive yet fearsome thing about prayer, *its authority*.

Prayer is a powerful thing. Prayer has already divided seas and rolled up flowing rivers, it has made flinty rocks gush into fountains, it has quenched flames of fire, it has muzzled lions, disarmed vipers and poisons, it has marshaled the stars against the wicked, it has stopped the course of the moon and arrested the sun in its orbit, it has burst open iron gates and recalled souls from eternity, it has conquered the strongest devils and commanded legions of angels down from heaven. Prayer has bridled and chained the raging passions of men and destroyed vast armies of proud, daring, blustering atheists. Prayer has brought one man from the bottom of the sea and carried another in a chariot of fire to heaven. This is not mere hyperbole; it is Scriptural fact!

Prayer has done a great many things for tens of thousands of Christians yet to be disclosed. It is an awesome, mighty force in the world of men and of Saints!

"Be still and know that I am God." (Psalm 46:10)

Why We Pray

In 685 AD, a man known as John of Beverley was made Bishop of Hexham. By any standards he was a remarkable person, overflowing with the Holy Spirit in such abundance that, according to legend, miracles occurred fairly regularly in his ministry. The key was his habit of taking time away from his active ministry to reflect and pray.

The Celtic Church was quite at ease with God intervening miraculously in the lives of the faithful. There was no sense of the dispensationalist, which says that the gifts of the Spirit are simply for the apostolic age. There was a very high expectation that holy people would be ready vehicles through which God could work powerfully.

The miraculous is closely linked with holiness and prayer. What we learn from the Celtic Church is that God's power moved through such men as John of Beverley, Aiden of Lindesfarne and Columba because they were deeply prayerful people. But we can too easily forget that we need to prepare ourselves in prayer and become open to God's power through living holy lives. As we know from St. Paul, it is possible to do all kinds of miraculous things without love but, in doing so, nothing is gained; "Though I speak with the tongues of men and of angels, and have not charity, I am become as sounding brass, or a tinkling cymbal. And though I have the gift of prophecy, and understand all mysteries, and all knowledge; and though I have all faith, so that I could remove mountains, and have not charity, I am nothing. And though I bestow all my goods to feed the poor, and though I give my body to be burned, and have not charity, it profiteth me nothing." (1 Cor 13:1-3)

Miracles in themselves have no great value. It is when they are connected to lives that transparently show the love of God, that they draw people into the kingdom of God. There is also no doubt that the Celtic Church believed deep intercessory prayer was needed for some healings, i.e. John of Beverly healing a priest called Heribald who fell from a horse with severe head injuries was up, around and completely healed the next morning.

It is most interesting that when church growth specialists such as Barna and Schaller looked at growing churches of all faiths in our day to see what made them so vital over the long term, one of the themes they persistently found over and over again WAS NOT a special elixir, a magic potion, a six piece ensemble with electric guitar or even an Alpha Program. They did find that those congregations that grew over a long period of time all had one thing in common; they accomplished a lot of praying. A wonderful re-discovery of the Celtic and Anglican traditions of the past two thousand years!!!! *And now it is our time to re-discover what is ours!*

Barna and Schaller found that these vital, growing congregations prayed and taught biblical teachings about prayer; what it is, what is done through it and in it, methods of prayer and related devotions, and prayer in all settings. Church leaders modeled a life of prayer, turned to prayer, described prayer's role in their lives and in churchly happenings, and then trusted God to answer the prayers as God saw fit. They sought answers to prayer, they learned how to recognize answers, and they accepted and often even celebrated the answers, even when they were not what they were anticipating. They constantly asked people about their prayer life, and encouraged deeper involvement in prayer.

The life of prayer is just that important! It is imbedded in the most fundamental of our beliefs, in the most important of our Sacraments. For example, in the liturgy of Baptism we see the life of prayer in microcosm.

Baptism is a once-for-all event: *ephapax*. "For in that he died, he died unto sin once: but in that he liveth, he liveth unto God."(Rom 6:10)

The Baptismal liturgy embodies the spiritual life in miniature. In the early church baptisma meant far more than the term 'Baptism' now signifies. It described the entire rite of Christian initiation, incorporating a series of elements and culminating in the first Holy Communion.

First, there was the renunciation. The candidate strips off old clothes, faces west in the darkness, repudiates Satan and all his works, and then turns round to the light of the baptistery. He is then anointed with the oil of exorcism and approaches the waters.

Second, there was the drowning...the symbol of Christ's dying and rising. "Therefore we are buried with him by baptism into death: that like as Christ was raised up from the dead by the glory of the Father, even so we also should walk in newness of life."(Rom 6:4) "Buried with him in baptism, wherein also ye are risen with him through the faith of the operation of God, who hath raised him from the dead."(Col 2:12)

Third, the candidate was clothed in the baptismal robe. He puts on Christ. "For as many of you as have been baptized into Christ have put on Christ." (Gal 3:27)

Fourth, the newly baptized was signed with the Cross, for it is in Christ crucified that we find 'the Spirit and power.' "I thank my God always on your behalf, for the grace of God which is given you by Jesus Christ;" (1Cor 1:4)

The Fathers speak of the signing as the *sphragis*, a term used originally of the wax seal which was used to indicate possession of cattle. "From henceforth let no man trouble me: for I bear in my body the marks of the Lord Jesus." (Gal 6:17)

Fifth, the baptismal anointing took place. The symbolic oil of Chrism stresses our participation in Christ.

Sixth, the candidate was given a candle, the sign of Christ's resurrection light.

The classic three ways of the life of prayer are thus present in microcosm in the Baptismal Rite:
- The way of purgation
- The way of illumination
- The way of union

A man must die inwardly in the ground of the soul. "I protest by your rejoicing which I have in Christ Jesus our Lord, I die daily." (1Cor 15:31)

There is also clothing with Christ. In the Christian dwells Christ, the hope of glory, and every man is to become mature in Christ. "To whom God would make known what is the riches of the glory of this mystery among the Gentiles; which is Christ in you, the hope of glory: Whom we preach, warning every man, and teaching every man in all wisdom; that we may present every man perfect in Christ Jesus: "(Col 1:27-28)

Coming to fullness of life in him. "And ye are complete in him, which is the head of all principality and power: "(Col 2:10) the Christian has put on the new nature. "And have put on the new man, which is renewed in knowledge after the image of him that created him:" (Col 3:10)

Prayer too is an anointing of the Spirit. St. Paul says God anointed us and put the Spirit in our hearts. "Now he which stablisheth us with you in Christ, and hath anointed us, is God;"(2Cor 1:21) "But ye have an unction from the Holy One, and ye know all things." (1Jn 2:20)

All prayer is standing in the light of Christ. We are to be the light to the world. "Then spake Jesus again unto them, saying, I am the light of the world: he that followeth me shall not walk in darkness, but shall have the light of life." (John 8:12) "Ye are the light of the world. A city that is set on an hill cannot be hid." (Matt 5:14) We are to wear the spiritual armor of light. "The night is far spent, the day is at hand: let us therefore cast off the works of darkness, and let us put on the armour of light." (Rom 13:12) To be children of light. "For ye were sometimes darkness, but now are ye light in the Lord: walk as children of light:" (Eph 5:8) "Ye are all the children of light, and the children of the day: we are not of the night, nor of darkness." (1Thes 5:5) To walk in the light. "But if we walk in the light, as he is in the light, we have fellowship one with another, and the blood of Jesus Christ his Son cleanseth us from all sin." (1Jn 1:7) Which comes from God which is light. "This then is the message which we have heard of him, and declare unto you, that God is light, and in him is no darkness at all." (1Jn 1:5)

Men must either pray or faint; there is no other choice. The Lord puts it on an either/or basis. The question to each of our hearts is: Am I fainting? Am I losing hearing? Is life to me just the surface, no depth, dull and shallow? Am I bored, unchallenged, defeated? If so, we are not praying.

But, you might say, I am praying! I pray thirty minutes every morning and ten minutes every night and I am even one of the few who attend (fill in the blank) weekday morning Mass as often as possible, but still life is not satisfying to me. I am not really living. Or perhaps you are among those of us who must hang our heads when the subject of prayer is brought up. In honesty we must say there is very little prayer in our life. We find it hard going to prayer and it is easy to forget or find something else to do.

At this point it would be very easy for me to thunder away at you with a campaign designed to put more prayer into your life. I could, I suppose, bring out some of the big guns of Scripture (which I will do for other reasons). Perhaps then some of us might go away resolved to try harder to schedule more prayer into everyday life. And if you did, I am sure it would not be long before you would be aware, as perhaps you already are, that this is not the final answer; that there is really nothing changed. Scheduling more time for prayer alone is not necessarily the answer.

Is it possible that our Lord is wrong here (as some of us may unconsciously be thinking) when he says, either pray or faint! Is it really that much of an issue? Are we not praying, and yet we faint? The problem is not that we need more of the same kind of prayer that we have been used to. What we need desperately to do is to discover the true nature of prayer.

For true prayer is not a difficult thing. It is natural, instinctive, and comes easily. This kind of prayer, Jesus says, is the key to God's power and glory.

> "And he spake this parable unto certain which trusted in themselves that they were righteous, and despised others: Two men went up into the temple to pray; the one a Pharisee, and the other a publican. The Pharisee stood and prayed thus with himself, God, I thank thee, that I am not as other men are, extortioners, unjust, adulterers, or even as this publican. I fast twice in the week, I give tithes of all that I possess. And the publican, standing afar off, would not lift up so much as his eyes unto heaven, but smote upon his breast, saying, God be merciful to me a sinner. I tell you, this man went down to his house justified rather than the other: for every one that exalteth himself shall be abased; and he that humbleth himself shall be exalted." (Luke 18:9-14)

Paul takes great pains to point out in the preceding parable that God is not like an unjust judge. God does not delay in answering prayer. But true prayer is, nevertheless, the only channel man has to the eagerness of God to help and bless us. Therefore Jesus provides the parable of the Pharisee and the publican, where he teaches the nature of authentic prayer.

As one minister who I respect categorizes it, we could call this parable, *The Parable of the Two Pray—ers* for it begins with these words, "Two men went up into the temple to pray." The object of our Lord in telling this parable is not to illustrate what self-righteousness is, though that is certainly involved, but he is still on the subject of prayer and he is telling us what real prayer is.

The Pharisee, in this little parable, was a man of prayer. He prays frequently, and punctiliously, without ever a miss. He was faithful in prayer, *but his prayer was entirely wrong.*

The publican, on the other hand, is not accustomed to praying. He is infrequently found in the temple courts. This is all new to him *but his prayer is exactly right.* As we watch these two portrayals let's understand the lessons Jesus intends.

In watching the Pharisee we learn what prayer is not. We learn there is a form of praying that is not prayer. This man assumed the correct posture for prayer. He stood, Jesus said, with his arms spread and his eyes uplifted unto heaven. Among the Jews, this was the prescribed posture for prayer. But, says Jesus, he prayed thus with himself! What a keen thrust that is! He was not praying to God, he was praying to himself! There was no one at the other end of the line. He was, perhaps, doing what some modern writers encourage, saying this is the true nature of prayer, that is, communing with the inner man. He certainly was not reaching any higher! He was not touching God; our Lord makes that point clear. Now what is this negative teaching about prayer?

First, it is clear that it is not prayer when we approach God impressed with our own virtues. This man stood and prayed, "God, I thank thee that I am not as other men are, extortionists, unjust, adulterers, or even like this publican…'" (Luke 18:11) He was obviously well impressed with what he felt were his claims upon God's attention. This man felt that God ought to be thanked for having made such a remarkable specimen of humanity, and if no one else will do it he will take on the task himself; that such an unusual man should not be left unacknowledged on the face of the earth. I am sure we could chuckle as we listen to his prayer, but do we not unconsciously reflect the same position?

The subject of prayer and healing has become of great interest to me over the past several years. I have made it an important study to read about and listen to Christians pray, including myself. It is frequently a very humorous experience and sometimes very sad.

Do we not often pray like this? *"Lord, won't you come and help me to do this task?"* We mean by this, *"I will contribute my ability to organize, my ability to exercise leadership, my talents for singing or speaking, and then, Lord, will you pour on the magic powder of Spirit-power, and you and I together will enjoy a great success."* In other words, we follow the philosophy in praying: "I'll do my best and let God do the rest." It isn't that we exclude him, and say, "I can do it all," but we say, "Lord, I have a part that I can contribute which you desperately need and I am willing to invest my two cents in this enterprise if you will do the rest. *You must do something, but I must do something too.*"

I submit to you that most Christian prayers are prayed from this basis. Sometimes the virtue that we plan to contribute to the program of God is that of *humility*. There is a kind of reverse brand of Pharisaic thought among Christians that goes something like this: "Thank God I am not as proud as this Pharisee is." And we make ourselves out to be utterly vile. We take the opposite position, we babble continually about our shortcomings and our sins. We say, "Lord, I am an extortionist, I am unjust, I take joy in destroying another's reputation, I admit it. I don't kid myself, I'm honest enough to admit that I am terrible." And thereby we hope to impress God with our honesty and our humility. Unfortunately, this pious form of reverse Pharisaic thought is found often among many Christians, perhaps not to such a degree, but of the same kind.

The simple truth is that we have no virtues of our own, none whatsoever. We have absolutely nothing to contribute to God's cause. We are praying out of utter bankruptcy, if we are honest with ourselves. We forget that these very talents with which we identify ourselves, these abilities that we have for leadership, or speaking, or singing, are in themselves gifts of God!

Is it not also strange how easily at times we identify ourselves with our virtues and disclaim identity with our faults? Our failures we blame on everyone else; for our successes we take full credit.

But there is so much that we forget.
- We forget God's shielding grace that has saved us from some of the terrible things others have fallen into for which we look down our nose at them.

- We forget that the only reason we are not standing in that poor wretch's shoes, who has been guilty of these vile and repulsive things, is simply because we have never been exposed to them. Are we sure we would not have fallen too, had we been there?
- We forget some of the things that are actually present in our lives. We forget our clever manipulations, our deliberate deceits, our put-on sympathies, and our dubious business arrangements. We are so careful to remember our values, our virtues, and our good points.

How do we get so well impressed with ourselves? Like this Pharisee we look downward from ourselves. He stood and saw, out of the corner of his eye, this tax collector, and immediately it made him virtuous. "Lord, I thank you I am not like that. I don't do any of those things." He had taken a vantage point that permitted him to look down on someone else. It is always possible to find someone who is lower down on the scale of human morals than we are, and what a comfort they are to our hearts! This is why many people love to gossip. What else explains this peculiar delight we take in sinking our teeth into someone else's reputation and slurping up the delicious tidbits of a deteriorating life? It is simply because it makes us feel superior. We delight in running someone else down because it makes us feel more virtuous. (A secret that political campaign planners use to manipulate us every 4 years! A little hatred here; a little self-righteousness there!)

This is the terrible point Jesus is making in describing the Pharisee. He says when we pray from this basis, when we approach God on this level, as we do so frequently, we are praying with ourselves. There is no real prayer; our pious words, and our properly phrased sentences, our completely scriptural, orthodox approach prayed from the Book of Common Prayer or Scriptural excerpts is of no value whatsoever. We are praying out of obsession with our own virtues. It is not that our Anglican prayer traditions are wrong…it is simply that *we are wrong*!

Furthermore, Jesus says, it is not prayer when we ask God's help because of our own accomplishments. The Pharisee expected God to act because he felt God could hardly do otherwise in view of the fine record of faithful service he laid before him. And do we not continually pray as though God owes us something? Listen to yourself pray:

- "Jesus, I have been faithfully tending to the development of our Anglican parish for several years. Surely now, Lord, you can do something for me."
- "Jesus, I have been trying to be a good Christian parent and have done my best, even teaching in the parish Sunday School, now please keep my children from going astray now that they have come into difficult times."
- "Jesus, I have given up so much for you, now give me this one little thing that I ask of you."

Obviously the Pharisee is still very much with us? "But," someone says, "does not Hebrews 6 say that God is not unrighteous to forget our labor of love?" Yes, it does, but, if we approach God on that basis, we have misunderstood the nature of prayer and we have missed the key to God's power.

There are rewards for believers, but not necessarily on this earth. The rewards here have to do with the strengthening of the inner life and not the carnal exterior. We must always consider ourselves unprofitable servants having done only that which is our duty to do. We have no claim on God by faithful service; it is only what we should have done. We have no right to come to him in prayer and demand that he answer because we have done this or that or another thing. This publican came into the temple and stood with his eyes cast down. He did not assume the posture of prayer; he was not even in the right place. All he could do was beat his breast and say, "God, be merciful to me, a sinner."

What do we learn about prayer from this man? Is it not obvious that real prayer, authentic prayer is an awareness of our helpless need? This man saw himself on the lowest possible level, a sinner. In fact, the original language is even stronger. He says, "God, be merciful to me the sinner;" the sinner, the very lowest kind, the worst kind. He believed that without God he could do absolutely nothing to help his position. I'm a sinner, Lord, that's all I can say. I have nothing else to add to it.

He does not say, "God be merciful to me a penitent sinner." He was penitent, but he does not urge that as any basis for God's blessing.

He does not say, "God be merciful to me a reformed sinner. I'm going to be different from now on." We many assume that he did do differently. We may assume that he stopped his extortion and cheating and his improper reporting, but he does not say "a reformed sinner," he does not urge this.

He does not even say, "God be merciful to me an honest sinner. Here I am, Lord, willing to tell you the whole thing. Surely you can't pass by honesty like that."

In fact, he does not even say, "God be merciful to me a *praying* sinner." He casts it all away. He says, "Lord, I haven't a thing to lean on but you."

How did he come to this place? He came exactly the reverse of the Pharisee. He did not look down on someone else below him **he looked up to God.** He judged upward, to God. He saw no one but God; he heard nothing but the high standard of God, "Love the Lord thy God with all thy heart and all thy soul and all thy strength and all thy mind," (Matt 22:37, Luke 10:37). "Lord, I'm the sinner. I'll never be any better in myself; I'm simply a sinner. I must have God, And in taking that place all that God had was available to him."

We are always to realize that we have no abilities in ourselves. We were never intended to feel adequate to meet any situation, apart from Jesus Christ. Prayer, therefore, is an expression of an awareness of helpless need that can only be met by God.

In this little book we learn a second thing about true prayer. Authentic prayer is always an acknowledgment of divine adequacy. Our help must be in God. This man looked for help nowhere else. He did not say, "Lord, perhaps this Pharisee standing here can help me." No, he said, "God be merciful to me." In that word *be merciful* is hidden all the wonderful story of the coming of Jesus Christ, the bloody cross, and the resurrection. This man used a theological word that means, "be propitiated to me," that is, "having had your justice satisfied, Lord, now show me thy love." And he believed that God's mercy was available, for, Jesus said, he "went down to his house justified." He was changed, he was different, and he was made whole. He laid hold of what God said, and believed him. And that too is what prayer is.

- Prayer is more than asking, *prayer is accepting*.
- Prayer is more than pleading, *prayer believes*.
- Prayer is more than words spoken, *it is a silent attitude maintained*.

Once we understand the very nature of true prayer then we may approach God, for whenever there is an awareness of need, that is an opportunity to let the heart, the thought, the voice, whatever form prayer may take, lift immediately to God, and say, "God, be merciful, Lord, I am a sinner. I desire your Will in my life. My hope, my help, my everything is in you for this moment." It does not matter whether it is only tying your shoes or washing the dishes, or writing a letter, or making a telephone call, whatever the need, that is the season for prayer.

Even after years of Christian life we can start again, and say, "Lord, this morning as I go out from this place of beautiful Anglican worship or I complete my morning prayers to You, let me consider your faithfulness to me, let me count upon your willingness to be in me and work through me as a member of this prayerful congregation to make my life all that it ought to be." Prayer is the breath and manifestation of the Spirit of love, and it finds its perfect expression in the Blessed Trinity. All genuine prayer has its source in the life of the Triune God.

If prayer is the breathing of the soul, and love its center, we may conclude that love is the source of prayer. Furthermore, genuine love refers to the selfless love that seeks the happiness of others and is not distorted by selfish passion or attachment. "Love is patient; love is kind; love is not envious or boastful or arrogant or rude. It does not insist on its own way; it is not irritable or resentful; it does not rejoice in wrongdoing, but rejoices in the truth. It bears all things, believes all things, hopes all things, and endures all things. Love never ends." (1Cor 13: 4-8).

Such love, true and eternal, cannot have a merely human origin. "Love is from God," says John the Apostle (1Jn 4:7). In the New Testament the word used for this love is agape (which differentiates it from Eros). St. Paul does not use agape to designate human love for God; he uses the phrase "to love God" only twice (Rom 8:28; 1Cor 8:3). The Christian love we call agape is essentially God's love for us manifested in Christ. Subsequently, this divine love that is transformed into love of neighbor is also agape. In the synoptic Gospels, however, the noun "agape" is seldom used: never in Mark, once each in Matthew (24:12) and Luke (11:42). The verb "to love" (agapao) is rarely used: eight times in Matthew, five times in Mark, thirteen times in Luke. Rather, it is God's love translated into action that permeates the entire Gospel, from first line to the last. "in this is love, not that we loved God, but that he loved us and sent his Son to be the atoning sacrifice for our sins" (1Jn 4:10). If we are capable of loving, it is because "[God] first loved us" (1Jn 4:19). When we say, "I want to pray," it is God who prays in us. It seems easier for us to say, "God loves" than "God prays." Yet, as St. Paul says, "the Spirit helps us in our weakness; for we do not know how to pray as we ought, but that very Spirit intercedes with sighs too deep for words" (Rom 8:26).

The word prayer generally evokes the image of petitions made to God, as in the second part of the Our Father, the Lord's Prayer. Yet hasn't God made it clear that before we pray for our "daily bread" we should first ask, "Hallowed by thy name, thy kingdom come"? Is not the petition "Your will be done on earth as it is in heaven" God's will for the establishment of his kingdom on earth, as well as an indication that the kernel of all prayer should be, before all else, a petition for God's kingdom and God's righteousness (Mt 6:33)? Viewed in this light, the heart of prayer lies not in God's response to our petitions but in making God's will our prayer. In other words, God's prayer should become the soul of our prayer. Because of our deafness and blindness, God's voice is often inaudible, so we lose sight of him and become like wandering sheep. We need, then, to pray for knowledge of God's will and for strength enlivened by God's prayer such is genuine prayer.

Figuratively speaking, prayer may be compared to water. God's prayer is the rain that comes from heaven. The land watered by this rain represents humanity. The water absorbed by the land eventually forms an underground current that later surfaces as a spring. Our prayer is this spring whose very existence depends on the rain, but if there is to be a spring, there must also be a center—a heart, that like the earth is capable of receiving and retaining the water from heaven, a heart that has emptied itself sufficiently to allow the underground current to flow freely into its empty space. In a heart that is hardened, attached to its own judgment, the spring of prayer will never be allowed to emerge. The basis for true prayer is to make God's will really ours before seeking to fulfill our own desires.

As we read in Ephesians, Christians were in danger of losing heart, losing love in their heart, the engine of prayer and the expression of faith. "Wherefore I desire that ye faint [lose heart] not at my tribulations for you, which is your glory." (Eph 3:13)

When an athlete is in an endurance contest of some kind, he presses on and on, though his legs begin to turn to rubber and his breath comes heavily and he experiences real physical pain. He keeps going nevertheless. And when he finishes, we say, "What a great heart he's got. He's got the morale, the stamina, to stay with it."

But when you lose heart you lose stamina, you lose morale. You come to the place where you say, "What's the use? Why keep going? I can't make it." And you give up. That is what Paul sensed was about to happen in Ephesus. They were about to give in, lose heart. So he says "I am concerned. Don't lose heart. The situation isn't the way you think it is." He teaches them some wonderful truth to show them why they should not to lose heart. But then he closes with this great prayer.

"For this cause I bow my knees unto the Father of our Lord Jesus Christ, Of whom the whole family in heaven and earth is named, That he would grant you, according to the riches of his glory, to be strengthened with might by his Spirit in the inner man; That Christ may dwell in your hearts by faith; that ye, being rooted and grounded in love, May be able to comprehend with all saints what is the breadth, and length, and depth, and height; And to know the love of Christ, which passeth knowledge, that ye might be filled with all the fullness of God." (Eph 3:14-19)

The apostle makes clear that they need not only to have light and knowledge to begin, but they need power to continue. They not only need motivation, but they need resolution to keep going to stay with it, to stick to the end. The above prayer is a prayer for power—power that keeps you going and helps you to recover from losing heart.

Why do we pray? Because God hears prayer and answers it.

Gen 20:17 "So Abraham prayed unto God: and God healed Abimelech, and his wife, and his maidservants; and they bare children."

1Ki 9:3 "And the LORD said unto him, I have heard thy prayer and thy supplication, that thou hast made before me: I have hallowed this house, which thou hast built, to put my name there for ever; and mine eyes and mine heart shall be there perpetually."

2Ki 20:5 "Turn again, and tell Hezekiah the captain of my people, Thus saith the LORD, the God of David thy father, I have heard thy prayer, I have seen thy tears: behold, I will

	heal thee: on the third day thou shalt go up unto the house of the LORD."
Ps 65:2	"O thou that hearest prayer, unto thee shall all flesh come."
Ps 66:19	"But verily God hath heard me; he hath attended to the voice of my prayer."
Ps 102:17	"He will regard the prayer of the destitute, and not despise their prayer."
Prov 15:29	"The LORD is far from the wicked: but he heareth the prayer of the righteous."
Phil 4:6	"Be careful for nothing; but in every thing by prayer and supplication with thanksgiving let your requests be made known unto God."
Js 5:16	"Confess your faults one to another, and pray one for another, that ye may be healed. The effectual fervent prayer of a righteous man availeth much."

Why do we pray? We pray because God commands us to pray.

Ps 32:6	"For this shall every one that is godly pray unto thee in a time when thou mayest be found: surely in the floods of great waters they shall not come nigh unto him."
1Sam 12:23	"Moreover as for me, God forbid that I should sin against the LORD in ceasing to pray for you: but I will teach you the good and the right way:"

Jer 29:11-13 "For I know the thoughts that I think toward you, saith the LORD, thoughts of peace, and not of evil, to give you an expected end. Then shall ye call upon me, and ye shall go and pray unto me, and I will hearken unto you. And ye shall seek me, and find me, when ye shall search for me with all your heart."

Why do we pray? We pray because our Lord himself taught us to pray.

Matt 5:44 "But I say unto you, Love your enemies, bless them that curse you, do good to them that hate you, and pray for them which despitefully use you, and persecute you

Matt 6:5-13 "And when thou prayest, thou shalt not be as the hypocrites are: for they love to pray standing in the synagogues and in the corners of the streets, that they may be seen of men. Verily I say unto you, They have their reward. But thou, when thou prayest, enter into thy closet, and when thou hast shut thy door, pray to thy Father which is in secret; and thy Father which seeth in secret shall reward thee openly. But when ye pray, use not vain repetitions, as the heathen do: for they think that they shall be heard for their much speaking. Be not ye therefore like unto them: for your Father knoweth what things ye have need of, before ye ask him. After this manner therefore pray ye: Our Father which art in heaven, Hallowed be thy name. Thy kingdom come. Thy will be done in earth, as it is in heaven. Give us this day our daily bread. And forgive us our debts, as we forgive our debtors. And lead us not into temptation, but deliver us from evil: For thine is the kingdom, and the power, and the glory, forever. Amen.

Luke 21:36 "Watch ye therefore, and pray always, that ye may be accounted worthy to escape all these things that shall come to pass, and to stand before the Son of man.

Jn 16:26-27 "At that day ye shall ask in my name: and I say not unto you, that I will pray the Father for you: For the Father himself loveth you, because ye have loved me, and have believed that I came out from God.

Why do we pray? We pray to remain in communion with Christ and his church.

Acts 1:14 "These all continued with one accord in prayer and supplication, with the women, and Mary the mother of Jesus, and with his brethren."

Acts 2:42 "And they continued steadfastly in the apostles' doctrine and fellowship, and in breaking of bread, and in prayers."

1Tim 2:1-8 "I exhort therefore, that, first of all, supplications, prayers, intercessions, and giving of thanks, be made for all men; For kings, and for all that are in authority; that we may lead a quiet and peaceable life in all godliness and honesty. For this is good and acceptable in the sight of God our Saviour; Who will have all men to be saved, and to come unto the knowledge of the truth. For there is one God, and one mediator between God and men, the man Christ Jesus; Who gave himself a ransom for all, to be testified in due time. Whereunto I am ordained a preacher, and an apostle, (I speak the truth in Christ, and lie not;) a teacher of the Gentiles in faith and verity. I will therefore that men pray every where, lifting up holy hands, without wrath and doubting.

Why do we pray? We pray because heaven is the kingdom of prayer in Jesus Christ.

Rev 5:8 "And when he had taken the book, the four beasts and four and twenty elders fell down before the Lamb, having every one of them harps, and golden vials full of odours, which are the prayers of saints."

"Hear my prayer, O LORD, and let my cry come unto thee."
(Ps 102:1)

How to Pray

Scripture leaves the Christian no doubt about the duty of prayer. "You ought always to pray, and not faint," our Lord said (Luke 18:1), and Paul exhorts, "pray without ceasing" (1Thess. 5:17).

Remember when Paul was converted on the Damascus Road? He had gone to Damascus breathing out threats and death against the Christians, and had already gained a reputation as the most violent and hostile persecutor of the Christians. Then he met Jesus Christ in the dust of the Damascus Road, and was led by the hand, blind and unseeing, into the city to wait there till someone should be sent by God to instruct him further as to what to do. Then it was, you remember, that the Spirit of God spoke to a man by the name of Ananias, and said, "And the Lord said unto him, Arise, and go into the street which is called Straight, and inquire in the house of Judas for one called Saul of Tarsus: for, behold, he prayeth," (Acts 9:11). Ananias objected, and said, "Lord, I have heard by many of this man, how much evil he hath done to thy saints at Jerusalem: And here he hath authority from the chief priests to bind all that call on thy name." (Acts 9:13-14). And you remember what God said, "behold, he prayeth," (Acts 9:11). In other words, this is the sign that he is now a believer, and he has yielded himself to Christ—*he prays.*

Prayer, I think, is the most distinctive mark of a Christian. If you don't pray, or have any desire for prayer, then it is very likely that is a sign that you are not a Christian at all, because, as the poet has put it, "Prayer is the Christian's native breath." We simply can't live as a Christian without praying—it is the simplest and best expression that we have of our sense of dependence upon God. Our dependence on God for all things fills the believer most especially in times of prayer; the recognition of such dependence is always fitting in the creature's relation to the creator, but especially in the sinner's relation to the Saviour. Paul emphasized this to the Colossians when he exhorted them to be "Giving thanks unto the Father, which hath made us meet to be partakers of the inheritance of the saints in light:"(Col. 1:12).

Prayer also is a joyful privilege. Coming as a beloved child to a loving Father is a happy situation in itself; more than that, however, when the loving Father is the God of Peace who has every reason to be the God of wrath, our invitation to appear before Him makes all earthly joys fade with the infinite wonder of such a privilege. According to Paul, when we come to the God of Peace in prayer "the peace of God, which surpasses all comprehension, shall guard your hearts and your minds in Christ Jesus" (Phil. 4:7,9).

Not only is prayer a duty as well as a privilege, in the providence of God it is effectual for the accomplishing of God's will. Paul's confidence of deliverance from prison rested on "your [the Philippians] prayers and the provision of the Holy Spirit" (Phil. 1:19). John reminded his beloved brethren of the confidence we may have that in *praying*, "according to His will...we have the request which we have asked of Him" (1Jn 5:14,15). James reminds us that "effectual prayer" accomplishes much (Js 5:16). Paul displays prayer as a part of the ongoing armor of the Christian in this life to be used for all saints and especially for those who preach the gospel. (Eph. 6:18-20).

> "And it came to pass, that, as he was praying in a certain place, when he ceased, one of his disciples said unto him, Lord, teach us to pray, as John also taught his disciples." (Luke 11:1)

This is a very significant request, because these disciples were undoubtedly already men of prayer. When they say to him, "Lord, teach us to pray, as John taught his disciples," they do not mean to imply that John had a superior school of ministry. They are not saying, "In that traveling seminary that John conducted he had a course on prayer, but you have not told us anything about this yet." What they mean is, "Some of us once were John's disciples and were taught by him how to pray, but Lord, we have been watching you, and we see that you are a master at prayer. Now as John once taught us how to pray, would you also impart to us the secrets of prayer? For, as we watch you, we see that the marvel and mystery of your character is linked with your prayer life, and it makes us aware how little we really know about prayer. Lord, would you teach us to pray?"

They saw first of all that, with Jesus, prayer was a necessity.

It was more than an occasional practice on his part it was a lifelong habit. It was an attitude of mind and heart. It was an atmosphere in which he lived; it was the very air he breathed. Everything he did arose out of prayer. He literally prayed without ceasing. The Apostle Paul urges us to pray without ceasing. As these disciples watched Jesus they saw that he was praying without ceasing.

Obviously it was not always formal prayer. He did not kneel every time, though he knelt sometimes. He did not stand with bowed head in an attitude of prayer continually. If he did, of course, he could not get anything done. The amazing thing is that he fulfilled his prayer life in the midst of an incredibly busy ministry

He was praying in spirit when his hands were busy healing. He gave thanks as he was breaking the bread and feeding the five thousand. At the tomb of Lazarus before he spoke those words, "Lazarus, come forth" (John 11:43b), in that dramatic display of power, he gave thanks to the Father openly. When the Greeks came and wanted to see Jesus, the message was brought to him and his immediate response was one of prayer, "Father," he said, "glorify Thy name," (John 12:28a). There was a continual sense of expectation that the Father would be working through him and thus he was praying by his attitude all the time.

This is the secret of prayer and of the prayer life. It is to practice this constant expectancy of attitude which means that we are never very far away from the thought that God is working in us both to will and to do of his good pleasure. He did this, of course, because he believed what he preached. He said continually, "The Son by himself can do nothing," (John 5:19). Those were not merely words; he was not mouthing pious phrases, as we frequently do. He was not trying to make a good impression on those around him. He was saying something that startled them, but he meant it, nevertheless. "The Son by himself can do nothing." Again and again he declared that to be true. "It is the Father who dwelleth in me, he doeth the works," (John 14:10b). And out of this conscious, constant sense of need there arose a continuing attitude of prayer, a continuing expectation that if anything is done, the Father would have to do it. This is what underlay his amazing prayer life, and revealed that to him prayer was an absolute necessity.

Now there is our problem! We have such an unexplainable attitude of self-sufficiency. Oh, there are times when we are conscious of our inadequacy, and our need, and are ready for prayer. Whenever you get down in the dumps, or are up against some circumstance that is tremendously demanding, or have been overwhelmed by some unexpected catastrophe, your first and automatic response is prayer. Why? Because you have a sense of need. You know you need help, and prayer is an automatic response at such times. But we think this is only emergency action reserved for those times when we are in great pressure or strain. For the rest of life we feel quite sufficient. We say, "There are lots of things I can do by myself. I'll pray when I need help, but the rest I can manage on my own." The secret of the life of Jesus is that he never said that, nor even once thought it. He never said to himself, "My training, my background, my knowledge, the ability that God has given to me as a man, make me sufficient for certain things on my own, the rest I'll depend on the Father for." No, he said, "The Son by himself can do nothing." Absolutely nothing!

This is one thing we must learn, that there is no activity of life that does not require prayer, a sense of expectation of God at work. Is not this what that disciple felt (it may even have been Peter) as he watched our Lord praying? He knew that, to him, prayer was an option. He prayed when he felt like it, he prayed when he thought it necessary, thinking that prayer was designed for emergency use only, for the "big" problems of life. Do we not need to begin right here? This phone call that I am about to make, I can't do it right except in prayer. It will never have the effect it ought to have except as my heart looks up to God and says "Speak through me in this." This letter I am about to write, this part I am making on the machine, how can I do it right, how can I fulfill my ministry except as I look to thee, Lord, to do it through me. "The Son by himself can do nothing," (John 5:19). This interview that I am about to conduct, this chart that I have to make for my studies, this report that I must turn in tomorrow, this room that I am sweeping, this walk I am going to take, this game I am about to play. These are the unending needs from which prayer rises.

Someone asked a dear cleaning lady what her method of prayer was, and she said, "I don't know nothin' about method. I just pray like this: When I wash my clothes, I pray, 'Lord, wash my heart clean.' When I iron them, I say, 'Lord, iron out all those troubles I can't do nothin' about.' When I sweep the floor, I say, 'Lord, sweep all the corners of my life like I'm sweepin' this floor.'"

The second thing this disciple saw in Jesus was that prayer was also perfectly natural.

There was no struggle on his part to pray. Prayer to him was not an act of self-discipline or duty; it was never duty, it was always delight. Now that does not mean that our Lord did not require time for prayer, nor that he did not have to arrange for prayer in his program. He had to make choices between other demanding things that threatened to consume his time. Sometimes we see him spend hours and whole nights in prayer. Occasionally he slipped away when the crowds were the very largest and the most demanding upon him. Luke records that a great multitude came together to hear him but he withdrew himself to a desert place and prayed. Sometimes it meant for him thanksgiving. You have such a prayer in Chapter 10 of Luke in Verses 21 and 22;

> "In that hour Jesus rejoiced in spirit, and said, I thank thee, O Father, Lord of heaven and earth, that thou hast hid these things from the wise and prudent, and hast revealed them unto babes: even so, Father; for so it seemed good in thy sight. All things are delivered to me of my Father: and no man knoweth who the Son is, but the Father; and who the Father is, but the Son, and he to whom the Son will reveal him."

He was always giving thanks. He was forever saying, "Thank you, Father. Thank you for the circumstance into which you have brought me, thank you for what you have planned to do about it, thank you for the victory that will be won through these circumstances, thank you for the needs that are being met." As he broke the bread to feed the five thousand he lifted his eyes and said, "Thank you, Father," (Matt 14:19). At the Last Supper as he gathered with his own in the Upper Room he took the cup and when he had given thanks he said, "Take, eat," (Matt 26:26, Mark 14:22). And all through his life prayer was thanksgiving.

Sometimes prayer was seeking counsel from the Father.

On the occasion when he was about to choose his disciples we are told he spent all the previous night in prayer.

Prayer for Jesus was frequently intercession.

We have the great account of it in John 17, that mighty prayer in which he prayed for the entire eleven apostles and through them for the whole church to every succeeding age. "I pray not for the world," he said, "but I pray for these and those who will hear my word through them," (John 17:20). He prayed for Peter in the hour of his disillusionment and defeat when his world came crashing around his head in the dark, dark night when he denied his Lord and went out and wept bitterly. The Lord had met him before and said, "Peter, I have prayed for thee that thy faith fail not," (Luke 22:32). Both Judas and Peter that night denied their Lord but the fundamental difference between Judas and Peter was that Christ had prayed for Peter. He prayed for the little children and made intercession for them with the Father. And finally, his great prayer of intercession was prayed on the bloody cross when his arms were stretched out. He prayed as they hammered the nails home in his flesh, "Father, forgive them, for they know not what they do," (Luke 23:34).

And then, supremely, prayer was communion to Jesus.

He prayed on the Mount of Transfiguration, and, as his disciples watched him, he was suddenly transformed before them. As he was praying, the countenance of his face was altered, and his garments became white and shining. In prayer he was experiencing a communion so rich that the glory of the Father that dwelt within him broke through the tent in which it was hidden. As John says, "We beheld his glory as of the only Begotten of the Father, full of grace and truth," (John 1:14).

Why do we struggle so, then? Why are we suddenly so busy when the prayer group meeting or the scheduled rosary group is brought up? Why do we piously favor prayer in general and devilishly resist it in particular?

The truth is, as we have been suggesting all along, that we are always in need, whether we feel it or not. When we think that everything is fine, that we need no help from God and that life is under control, we are suffering from a satanic delusion, a fantasy, a bubble of imagination that is bound ultimately to burst in confusion. Life is really under control only when our attitude is what Jesus' attitude was, one of continual need and constant expectation. God is always the same, and on that great unshakable rock faith continually rests and continually looks for continual supply. We are to be continually accepting, he is forever giving. Giving is his job, ours is to receive.

Prayer then is to be our life and our breath so that no one need urge us to pray anymore than they would urge us to breathe or to eat. We know we must pray.

If we were honest we'd probably all say there are thousands of prayers that go up but there are very few answers that come down. Why is that? What causes that? Is prayer a farce, a superstition, something we just con ourselves into and pretend that it works but it really doesn't? What is prayer?

There's a deeper question than that. Does God promise to answer everyone's prayers?

No! It's very clear in scripture that God completely ignores some people's prayers. In fact, the Bible says that God has laid out some conditions to answered prayer. I want us to look at those conditions because until you meet the conditions for answered prayer, you're wasting your breath.

If you meet these conditions you may expect that what you ask for will be answered in prayer.

1. You must have an honest relationship to God.

"If ye abide in me, and my words abide in you, ye shall ask what ye will, and it shall be done unto you."(John 15:7) That's a beautiful promise. But in Scripture every promise has a condition or every promise has a premise. The promise here is, "I will give you whatever you ask in prayer if you remain in Me." In other words, "…if you have a honest relationship with Me."

How do you remain in Christ? The next sentence tells it, by my words remaining in you. In other words, God says if we fill our minds with the Bible, the word of God, then we will be in Christ. We will be abiding in Him. God requires that we listen to Him first before He listens to us. If I don't pay attention to what God says to me in His word, why should He pay attention to me when I talk to Him? If I ignore His word, why should He pay attention to what I say to Him?

The starting point is that you have an honest relationship to God. How? You begin with Word of God. That's why Scripture study with your priest is important. You think, "Are you saying if I don't study Scripture I won't have answered prayer?" No, what I am saying is your prayer life will never be more effective than how much you understand Scripture. The more you understand the Bible the more you'll know how to pray effectively.

Three questions on how to evaluate if you have an honest relationship to God. 1 John gives us evaluative questions to determine our relationship to God.

- **"That which was from the beginning, which we have heard, which we have seen with our eyes, which we have looked upon, and our hands have handled, of the Word of life;" (I Jn 1:1)**

Have I refused to admit things that I have done wrong in the past? The Bible says that's called un-confessed sin. It may be an activity, an attitude, or a habit. When we go our own way, do our own thing; it breaks the connection between God and us. When we try to cover up things that we know are wrong from God then that honest relationship is broken. There's falseness, a con, a fraud, trying to live two different lives at once—live for God and live for myself. So the first thing I ask if I'm really being honest with God is have I admitted what I've done wrong.

Psalm 66:18 says "If I regard iniquity in my heart, the Lord will not hear me:" Isaiah 59:2 says "But your iniquities have separated between you and your God, and your sins have hid his face from you, that he will not hear." Proverbs 28:13 says "He that covereth his sins shall not prosper: but whoso confesseth and forsaketh them shall have mercy."

What do you do? 1 John 1:8-9 "If we say that we have no sin, we deceive ourselves, and the truth is not in us. If we confess our sins, he is faithful and just to forgive us our sins, and to cleanse us from all unrighteousness." What is confession? Confession is simply being honest with God. It's saying, "God, You're right. I was wrong. That jealousy or that impatience was wrong. Please forgive me." The first way we can tell if we have an honest relationship with God is are we being honest when we make mistakes. "God, You're right. That was a mistake. That was wrong. It was an error."

- **"Beloved, if our heart condemn us not, then have we confidence toward God. And whatsoever we ask, we receive of him, because we keep his commandments, and do those things that are pleasing in his sight." (I Jn 3:21-22)**

Am I currently in the present ignoring any of God's principles? In other words, when God tells me to do something, when I know I'm holding on to something that God wants me to let go of and I continue to hold on to it, that breaks the prayer chain, the connection with God.

You think, "How can I keep all of God's commands?" Nobody's perfect. "How am I ever going to get any answers?" God does not demand perfection. He simply demands obedience. And obedience is an attitude: I want to do what's right. God doesn't expect perfection, but He does expect you to obey.

Example: I tell my thirteen-year-old daughter, Katherine, "Please go clean up your room." If thirty minutes later I go in and the room is fairly well picked up although she's still got things piled on her chair—it's not immaculate, do I get upset about it? No. She's not perfect; she did the best she could. But if I come in a half hour later and she's still watching an English comedy on TV, then do I get upset? Yes! Why? Because as a parent, I don't expect perfection but I do expect obedience, an attitude of "I want to do what's right."

So we ask, "Am I hiding something from God in my relationship?... Am I doing what I know He wants me to do at this point?"

- **"And this is the confidence that we have in him, that, if we ask any thing according to his will, he heareth us: And if we know that he hear us, whatsoever we ask, we know that we have the petitions that we desired of him."(I Jn 5:14-150)**

Do I really want God's will for my life? When we ask according to God's will then we have confidence in prayer and we know He's going to answer.

Most Christians make a big mistake in prayer. They go around constantly saying, "God, is it your will that I ask for this?" over every little item. The real issue is not "God, what is your will regarding this specific circumstance?" The real issue is "Am I in God's will as a person?" If my life is in harmony with God, then my desires are going to be in harmony with God.

St. Augustine said this: "Love God and do what you please." Why did he say that? He said it because, if you really love God with all your heart, you're not going to want to do what displeases God.

In his *Letters of Saint Augustine, Letter CXXX, Chapter X* AD412 we read

"Wherefore it is neither wont nor unprofitable to spend much time in praying, if there be leisure for this without hindering other good and necessary works to which duty calls us, although even in the doing of these, as I have said, we ought by cherishing holy desire to pray without ceasing. For to spend a long time in prayer is not, as some think, the same thing as to pray 'with much speaking.' Multiplied words are one thing; long-continued warmth of desire is another. For even of the Lord Himself it is written, that He continued all night in prayer.

'And it came to pass in those days, that he went out into a mountain to pray, and continued all night in prayer to God.'(Luke 6:12)

And that His prayer was more prolonged when He was in an agony;....

'And he was withdrawn from them about a stone's cast, and kneeled down, and prayed, Saying, Father, if thou be willing, remove this cup from me: nevertheless not my will, but thine, be done. And there appeared an angel unto him from heaven, strengthening him. And being in an agony he prayed more earnestly: and his sweat was as it were great drops of blood falling down to the ground.' (Luke 22:41-44)

…And in this is not an example given to us by Him who is in time an Intercessor such as we need, and who is with the Father eternally the Hearer of prayer?"

The brethren in Egypt are reported to have very frequent prayers, but these very brief, and, as it were, sudden and ejaculatory, lest the wakeful and aroused attention which is indispensable in prayer should be protracted exercises vanish or lose its keenness. And in this they themselves show plainly enough, that just as this attention is not to be allowed to become exhausted if it cannot continue long, so it is not to be suddenly suspended if it is sustained. Far be it from us either to use 'much speaking' in prayer, or to refrain from prolonged prayer, if fervent attention of the soul continue…pray in hope, pray in faith, pray in love, pray earnestly and patiently…"

So you don't have to constantly say, "Is it your will?" You go down to buy a new car: "God is it your will that I buy a brown Chevy or a gold Mercedes?…God, is it your will that I order the steak or the pork chops—give me a sign?" No, you should not ask God's will on every little item like that. You get your life in God's will and say, "To the best of my knowledge, I'm trying to do what's right, Lord. I want to live in your will." Then you ask according to your desires.

How do you know the answer to the question, "Do I really want God's will for my life?" How do you know if you really want it? Simple. How eager are you to read Scripture? Because the only way you can know the will of God is by reading the word of God. And God's word tells you God's will. So you want to read it, you want to study it.

So the first condition to answered prayer is this: You have an honest relationship to God.

2. You must have a forgiving attitude toward other people

"Therefore I say unto you, What things soever ye desire, when ye pray, believe that ye receive them, and ye shall have them. And when ye stand praying, forgive, if ye have ought against any: that your Father also which is in heaven may forgive you your trespasses."(Mark 11:24-25)

More than any other characteristic in the Bible except faith, the number one thing related to prayer is forgiveness. Over and over again, every time Jesus talks about prayer He talks about forgiveness. Why? Because Christ knows that resentment will destroy your prayers more quickly than any other sentiment! When you hold a grudge, when you nurse an ill feeling, when you allow bitterness to grow in your life, it destroys your prayers. Maybe you're praying and not getting an answer because you're holding a grudge against somebody…even yourself!

In Matthew 5, Jesus giving the Sermon on the Mount, He says when you go to church and you're going to offer a gift to the Lord and you remember that you've got something against somebody or they've got something against you, stop, leave the gift right there at the church, go out, find that person, get forgiveness or offer forgiveness, make harmony in the relationship if you can, then come back and continue giving your gift to the Lord. Why? Because God says you can't say you love God and hate your brother. One of the primary reasons why people never see answers to prayer is because they allow bitterness to spring up in their lives.

"Looking diligently lest any man fail of the grace of God; lest any root of bitterness springing up trouble you, and thereby many be defiled;" (Heb 12:15) Bitterness is like a poison, it will eat you alive. You cannot be unforgiving in your heart and have your prayers answered.

What do you pray every time you pray the Lord's Prayer? "Father, forgive us our trespasses and we forgive those who trespass against us." You're saying, "God, I want you to forgive me as much as I forgive everybody else." Do you really want to pray that? "God, You forgive me as much as I forgive everybody else." Why? Bitterness and resentment will block prayer.

We read in the *Epistle of Ignatius to the Ephesians, Chapter IX AD 107* "And pray ye without ceasing in behalf of other men. For there is in them hope of repentance, that they may attain to God."

1 Peter 3:7 expresses why sometimes you haven't had an answer to prayer. Peter is talking about marriage. Did you know that one of the easiest places to have resentment build up is in the family? Family members hurt each other's feelings, husbands hurt wives, wives hurt husbands, parents hurt their children and vice versa. Bitterness and resentment are a common experience in family relationships. Peter has given the low-down to the women then in verse 7 he starts talking to the husbands. He says "Likewise, ye husbands, dwell with them according to knowledge, giving honour unto the wife, as unto the weaker vessel, and as being heirs together of the grace of life; that your prayers be not hindered."

Did you know that the Bible says that disharmony in the home blocks answers to prayer? That's why some people don't have answers to prayer. In fact the Scripture says how you treat your spouse influences your prayer life. That's pretty strong. In the Scriptures, when it lists the qualifications that a priest must have in his life in order to be a priest, one of the qualifications is he has to have a happy, peaceful home life. Why? Because if you're in tension at home, the prayers of those leaders of the church will be totally ineffective according to Scripture.

3. You must be willing to share the results

This is the principle of "What you sow you reap," "Give and it will be given unto you." It's the principle of generosity; the more you give out, the more God gives to you. If you expect God to bless your life you must be willing to bless other people's lives with the same benefits God has given to you.

Proverbs 21:13 "Whoso stoppeth his ears at the cry of the poor, he also shall cry himself, but shall not be heard." That's a fact of life. God says if you pay no attention to other people's legitimate needs, why should He pay attention to your needs? He wants us to be like Him. He says a prerequisite for God to bless our lives is that we must be blessings to other people. If we ignore those who are in obvious difficulty around us, what right do we have to expect God to bail us out?

In 1Jn 3:22 we've read the verse that says "And whatsoever we ask, we receive of him, because we keep his commandments, and do those things that are pleasing in his sight." We receive from Him anything we ask because we obey His commands." What are His commands? The next verse: "And this is his commandment, That we should believe on the name of his Son Jesus Christ, and love one another, as he gave us commandment."

He says one of the ways we keep commands is by loving other people. What is He talking about? v. 17 "But whoso hath this world's good, and seeth his brother have need, and shutteth up his bowels of compassion from him, how dwelleth the love of God in him?" One of the ways we prove that we have love is we're willing to be generous with other people. God blesses us so that we may bless others. This is the principle of stewardship. It's all through scripture—that God blesses us in order that we might be blessings to other people.

We are channels. I would not presume to ask God to bless my parish if I were not willing to at least give back a portion of what He had blessed me in a percentage, a tithe. You say, "I ask God for good health." What are you going to do with that healthy body after you've got it? Are you going to spend all the effort and energy on yourself or are you willing to help other people? One of the conditions for answered prayer is to be willing to help those less fortunate with the blessings of which we are blessed.

In James 4:1 we read, "From whence come wars and fightings among you? come they not hence, even of your lusts that war in your members?" You want something but you don't get it. You kill and you covet but you can't have what you want. You quarrel and you fight. But you have not because you don't ask God…v. 3 gives us another reason why our prayers are hindered: "Ye ask, and receive not, because ye ask amiss, that ye may consume it upon your lusts." He's saying motive is important in prayer. How you pray is more important than what you pray for.

Is it possible to pray for the right thing with the wrong motive? Sure. Should you never pray for your own personal needs? I'm not saying that. Jesus says to pray for your own needs. He says to pray, "Give us this day our daily bread." In Mark 11, He says you can even pray for your desires. But the motive is, are you willing to share your blessing with other people or are you going to horde it all to yourself?

> We read in *The Treatises of Cyprian; Treatise IV, On the Lord's Prayer*, AD258;
> "But let our speech and petition when we pray be under discipline, observing quietness and modesty. Let us consider that we are standing in God's sight. We must please the divine eyes both with the habit of body and with the measure of voice…
>
> Moreover, in His teaching the Lord has bidden us to pray in secret—in hidden and remote places, in our very bed-chambers—which is best suited to faith, that we may know that God is everywhere present, and hears and sees all, even into hidden and secret places, as it is written….
> 'Am I a God at hand, saith the LORD, and not a God afar off? Can any hide himself in secret places that I shall not see him? saith the LORD. Do not I fill heaven and earth? saith the LORD.' (Jer 23:23-24)
>
> 'The eyes of the LORD are in every place, beholding the evil and the good' (Prov 15:3)

Before all things, the Teacher of peace and the Master of unity would not have prayer to be made singly and individually, as for one who prays to pray for himself alone....Our prayer is public and common; and when we pray, we pray not for one, but for the whole people, because we the whole people are one... "

God is not interested in simply satisfying our selfishness. The conditions of prayer are one, an honest relationship to God; two, a forgiving attitude toward other people; three, a willingness to share God's blessings to us with other people.

> We read in *Origen's Second Book of the Commentary on the Gospel According to Matthew,* Book XIV, Part I, The Power of Harmony in Relation to Prayer, AD248
>
> "...for the instruments thus fitted with might and with songs, had in themselves the musical symphony which is so powerful that when two only, bring along with the symphony which has a relation to the music that is divine and spiritual, a request to the Father in heaven about anything whatsoever, the Father grants the request to those who ask along with the symphony on earth... But perhaps also not even few but two or three make a symphony as Peter and James and John, to whom as making a symphony the Word of God showed His own glory."

In the Celtic church even the hermits who practiced quiet, reclusive meditative prayer (which we will study later), never thought that they were alone but rather completely connected to all. He or she was part of the monastic community. They clearly saw themselves as having an intercessory responsibility for the nation. After a victory against the ever-threatening Penda, King Oswy gave twelve grants of land where, as expressed by Bede, "heavenly warfare was to take the place of earthly." To turn a battle site into a place of prayer was typical of the Celtic desire to heal the land, to turn darkness to light.

If you want God to bless you, you must be willing to be a channel of blessing to other people.

4. You must believe that God will answer

"If any of you lack wisdom, let him ask of God, that giveth to all men liberally, and upbraideth not; and it shall be given him. But let him ask in faith, nothing wavering. For he that wavereth is like a wave of the sea driven with the wind and tossed. For let not that man think that he shall receive any thing of the Lord." (James 1:5-7) He says, If you need any wisdom go ahead and ask God and He will give it to you. He's not going to complain. You don't have to convince Him.

The fourth condition for answered prayer is that you must believe that God will answer. You can't doubt. You must expect God to answer. There's only one kind of prayer that God answers: the prayer of faith. In Mark 9:29 we read "And he said unto them, This kind can come forth by nothing, but by prayer and fasting." What are you expecting God to do in your life? In Hebrews 11:6 we read "But without faith it is impossible to please him: for he that cometh to God must believe that he is, and that he is a rewarder of them that diligently seek him." You can't even please God if you don't have faith. It's the number one pre-requisite in life. Have faith.

> The Jewish Chassidic teachings, our heritage, are particularly relevant here (2.1)

"A person may have prayed profusely and secluded himself with God day after day for years and years and still feel that he is very far from God. He may even start to think that God is hiding His countenance from him. But it is a mistake if he thinks that God does not hear his prayers. He must believe with perfect faith that God pays attention to each and every word of every single prayer, petition and conversation. Not a single word is lost, God forbid. Each one leaves its mark in the worlds above, however faintly. Little by little they awaken God's love. If there seems to be no response, the reason is that as yet the holy edifice he is destined to enter is not yet complete. The main thing is not to give up and fall into despair. This would be foolish. Be firm and continue with your prayers with new determination. In the end God's love will be aroused and He will turn to you and shine His radiance upon you and fulfill your wishes and desires through the strength of the true Tzaddikim. He will draw you towards Himself in love and abundant mercy."

What is faith? Does faith believe that God can do it? "I believe God can do it!" That's not faith.

When you believe God can, that's just a fact. God can do it whether you believe it or not. "I believe God might do it." That's not faith either. That's hope. You hope He might.

"I believe God will do it." That's faith. Not believing God can do it, not believing God might do it, but believing God will do it. Faith! We read in *The Pastor of Hermas, Book Second—Commandments, Commandment Ninth—Prayer must be made to God without ceasing, and with unwavering confidence.* AD160;

"Cleanse your heart, therefore, from all doubt, and put on faith, because it is strong, and trust God that you will obtain from Him all that you ask…Wherefore, do not cease to make the request of your soul, and you will obtain it."

Faith is not desire. Some people think, "I've got this tremendous desire. I've got these goals that I'm praying about—family goals, spiritual goals, financial goals, health goals. I'm praying about all these goals. I really have a desire." Desire is not faith. Desire can lead to faith but it's not faith.

I honestly believe that if God actually answered some people's prayers they'd have a heart attack. An answered prayer! He probably hasn't answered some of them to keep them alive! "They don't believe I'm going to do it, so I might as well not." We see so little in our lives because we expect so little in our lives. The Scripture states "According to your faith" not according to your ability, not according to your education, not according to how good a person you are but "According to your faith, it will be done unto you."

The fact is, if you have met the conditions of Scripture—you have an honest relationship to God, you have, as far as you know, no unforgiving attitude toward anyone, you're willing to share the results with other people, and you're asking God in faith and expecting—in our Jewish heritage, you have every right to expect God to answer.

5. You must pray in Jesus' name

"Hitherto have ye asked nothing in my name: ask, and ye shall receive, that your joy may be full." (John 16:24) The fifth condition for answered prayer—you must pray in Jesus' name.

What is so special about Jesus' name? Some people think "In Jesus' name" is kind of a mystical password that gets you into God. Is there a secret formula, a word? "Here are all my requests; by the way—codeword "In Jesus' name!" What in the world does it mean to pray "In Jesus' name"? What does it mean?

I heard a story once that illustrates it. A pastor took his young son and several of his son's friends to the carnival for a birthday party. He bought a roll of tickets and stood at the front of every ride and as the kids came by. He gave everybody a ticket. He was just handing them out. All of a sudden he looked up and realized there was a little boy with his hand out asking for a ticket that he'd never seen in his life. He stopped and said, "Son, are you with my son's party?" No." "Why should I give you a ticket?" The young boy turned around and pointed to the man's son and said, "Your son said you'd give me one." So he gave him one.

Here's the point. I don't have any right to get any answered prayers from God. What makes me think I should have my prayers answered? God doesn't owe me anything. I owe him a lot but He doesn't owe me anything. When I come and pray and ask God for requests, I don't ask on my own merit but I come on the merit of Christ. I come and say, "Father, I'm coming to you because Your Son said so. I'm coming because what Jesus Christ has already done for me on the cross and He's promised and He said I could ask in His name. God, I'm coming in Jesus' name."

> We read in St. Augustine's *Tractates on the Gospel of St. John*, Tractate X, Chapter II: 12-21, AD418;
>
> "There is one that heareth prayer, hesitate not to pray; but He that heareth abideth within. You need not direct your eyes towards some mountain; you need not raise your face to the stars, or to the sun, or to the moon; nor must you suppose that you are heard when you pray beside the sea: rather detest such prayers. Only cleanse the chamber of your heart; whersoever thou art, wherever thou prayest, He that hears is within, within the secret place, which the psalmist calls his bosom..
>
> 'But as for me, when they were sick, my clothing was sackcloth: I humbled my soul with fasting; and my prayer returned into mine own bosom.' (Ps 35:13)"

Jesus is the bridge between God and man. God came in the form of a man—Jesus Christ. Jesus said it like this, "I am the Way. No one comes to the Father except through Me." Let's say I was to go to the bank. I walk into the bank where I've never been before in my life and pull out my checkbook, write out a check for cash for $1000 and sign it in my name. I hand the check to the teller. She looks at it and recognizes that it's not from her bank and she says, "Father Sokol, do you have an account at our bank?" I say, "No." She says, "I'm sorry. I can't accept this check. It's in your name but you don't have an account here." Now let's say that I have a very wealthy friend. We go in together. He walks up to the teller and says, "Give my friend what he needs." He pulls out his checkbook, writes a check to Rev. Sokol and signs it *in his name* and hands it to her. Immediately my transaction is answered. My friend commands a credit line that I will never know.

Jesus Christ has the relationship with the Father that I will never know. Where I may be spiritually bankrupt, He is everything. When I come to God and pray, "In Jesus' name" I'm saying, "God, I realize that you don't have any reason to give me this, but I'm coming in Jesus' name because of Him, because of what He's done."

Is it always necessary to say the word, "In Jesus' name" at the end of every prayer? I don't think it's necessary if you have the attitude, but I think it's a good idea. I don't see anything wrong with doing it every time. Why? Because it reminds you why you have the right to pray. It is a constant reminder. You don't have to say it at the end; you could say it at the start. "Lord, Father, I'm coming to you in Jesus' name." You don't have to tack it on at the end. But I think it's a good reminder of the fact that the way we pray is in Jesus' merit, not our own. We should pray to the Father, the Heavenly Father, through the Son.

Which of these conditions have you been overlooking and that's why you haven't been getting any answers to prayer?

- Maybe you've been holding a grudge. Maybe you've been nursing resentment and you have allowed bitterness to build up in your life and it's no wonder you don't have any answers to prayer.
- Maybe you've been refusing to admit some wrong in your life. You've known it was there but you didn't want to go to God and say, "You're right, God, that's wrong. I admit it." We think this political shenanigans or that one was a cover up. It's nothing compared to some of the things we try on God. So we say, "God, I admit it. That was wrong. I shouldn't have lost my cool just then."
- Maybe you've prayed but you've never really expected God to answer. If you don't expect God to answer, you're just wasting your time. Don't even pray. God says, "Why bother? If you don't believe that I'm going to do it, don't even make the effort." It's a condition.
- Maybe you've been unwilling to share God's blessing with other people. Maybe you've been hesitant to give back to God a percentage of all the things He's been blessing you with. You must be willing to share the benefits with other people.

If the above are true of you, then you haven't been abiding in Him, abiding in His word. Have you been praying in Jesus' name? You can't pray in Jesus' name unless you know Him as a friend, as your Lord, as your Saviour, as the director of your life. The most important question is, "Do you have an honest and loving relationship with God?" I'm not talking about membership in your parish. I'm not talking about being religious. I'm talking about a loving relationship with your Saviour.

The love relationship: an enduring, continuing, growing love relationship with God. An overwhelming love invites a response. Loving is the syntax of prayer. To be effective pray-ers, we need to be effective lovers. Scripture breathes the message of Divine Love. Real prayer comes from falling in love.

To pray is to change. This is a great grace. God provides a path whereby our lives can be taken over by love and joy and peace and patience and kindness and goodness and faithfulness and gentleness and self-control. That's why He sent Christ to earth, so we could know what Christ is like. Jesus said, "I am the Way." An abiding love provides for perpetual Grace and response to prayer.

"O LORD God of hosts, hear my prayer: give ear, O God of Jacob. Selah." (Ps 84:8)

Part Two:

Preparation for a Prayer-Filled Experience

The Preparation Process

"I pointed out how the devil then lies in wait, deceiver that he is. For since he sees very great gain accruing to us from prayer, then most he assails us, in order that he may disable us from our defense; that he may send us off home empty-handed.

Prayer with earnestness is a light of the understanding and soul—a light unquenchable and perpetual. On this account he throws into our minds countless rubbish-heaps of imaginations; and things which we never had imagined, these collecting together at the very moment of prayer he pours down upon our souls. And just as winds often rushing from an opposite quarter by a violent gust extinguish a lamp's flame as it is being lighted, so also the devil, when he has seen the flame of our prayer being kindled, blowing it on every side with the blasts of countless thoughts, does not desist before and until he has quenched the light." St. Chrysostom, *Homily Against Publishing the Errors of the Brethren*, AD398

Relationships do not develop smoothly. We prefer to avoid change, to re-calibrate our 'categories' of life and love. But, at the same time we are want for change. We do not want to be bored but look for the development of existing relationships or the establishment of new ones. Our natural tendencies overflow into our life of prayer as well. Satan surely enjoys exploiting our immaturity in prayer caused by our lack of reconciliation to our Lord.

Let's listen to a whimsical communication between a trainer of devils and a neophyte tempter. We read...

"My dear Wormwood. The best thing, where it is possible, is to keep the patient from the serious intention of praying altogether. When the patient is an adult recently reconverted to the Enemy's party....this is best done by encouraging him to remember, or to think he remembers, the parrot like nature of his prayers in childhood. In reaction against that, he may be persuaded to aim at something entirely spontaneous, inward, informal, and without regulation; and what this will actually mean to a beginner will be an effort to produce in himself a vaguely devotional mood in which real concentration of will and intelligence have no part. One of their poets, Coleridge, has recorded that he did not pray "with moving lips and bended knees" but merely "composed his spirit to love: and indulged "a sense of supplication." That is exactly the sort of prayer we want; and since it bears a superficial resemblance to the prayer of silence as practiced by those who are very far advanced in the Enemy's service, clever and lazy patients can be taken in by it for quite a long time. At the very least, they can be persuaded that the bodily position makes no difference to their prayers; for they constantly forget, what you must always remember, that they are animals and that whatever their bodies do affects their souls. It is funny how mortals always picture us as putting things into their minds: in reality our best work is done by keeping things out.

If this fails, you must fall back on a subtler misdirection of his intention. Wherever they are attending to the Enemy Himself we are defeated, but there are ways of preventing them from doing so. The simplest is to turn their gaze away from Him toward themselves........

...If you examine the object to which he is attending, you will find that it is a composite object containing many quite ridiculous ingredients. There will be images derived from pictures of the Enemy as He appeared during the discreditable episode known as the Incarnation: there will be vaguer—perhaps quite savage and puerile—images associated with the other two Persons...I have known cases where what the patient called his "God" was actually located—up and to the left at the corner of the bedroom ceiling, or inside his own head, or in a crucifix on the wall. But whatever the nature of the composite object, you must keep him praying to it...not to the Person who has made him...

Your affectionate uncle
SCREWTAPE"

C. S. Lewis, *The Screwtape Letters*, Letter IV, Colliers Books, Riverside, NJ, Revised 1982

Satan does not appear in our everyday lives through massive displays of pyrotechniques, or on one of the four horses of the apocalypse, or even as that dark, ominous shadow in the corner. That is all Hollywood and quite unreal. Satan knows, as our Lord has taught, that all of life, love and Faith occur in the small and sometimes insignificant (to us for the moment) elements of everyday life.

1. **Understand your perception and emotions toward God.**

Let's take a moment to consider any manifestations of resistance to prayer; the path to our Lord that you may have experienced. *After you read the listing below jot down an immediate, private response about you.*

Is it possible that any of the following describe you and your prayer life? How?

- Blindness to certain facets of life or the obvious meaning of a text of Scripture.
- Persistent repetition of the same pattern of response.
- Falling asleep in prayer can be a sign of massive resistance of meeting the Holy One. This is similar to an individual facing highly charged and stressful situations on the job or at home...and finding that they fall into sleep (avoidance) more often than previously.
- Doubts about the reality of prayer and the possibility of ever knowing whether one has experienced God can be manifestations of resistance...skipping morning or evening prayers, deciding not to attend a prayer group after joining, etc.
- Fear of God (putting God in a box) with such statements as 'why should I confess if God knows everything? Or 'God can't ask the impossible of a person!' Although a grain of truth in both....the important point is that it is pushed forward as a defense mechanism.
- Fear of confronting THE SECRET. There may be something that a person does not want the Lord...or maybe themselves to 'know.' Sometimes it is necessary to share the SECRET with another trusted friend before gaining the courage to share it ...to give it...to the Lord.

- Take a moment to recollect your weaknesses that may be addressed above or any others brought to mind. Jot them down below (privately), as you will want to revisit these issues with your Lord momentarily. OK. Now, your thoughts about you!

2. **Now, visualize your present relationship to the Lord.**

We have four categories of knowing others.

- Neutral Objects—descriptions through third parties of those we have never met.
- Acquaintances—Those we have met, may know a little something about (usually in one limited 'public' arena...such as strictly a work relationship, a neighbor that we meet in passing as we walk our dogs, smile and say hello, etc.) and may see again, but usually by chance encounter, or at scheduled encounters with very limited interaction (belonging to the same committee, civic group, etc.)

- Friends—Those who we know more about (husband, wife, children, background, etc.) and who know something about us. They tend to be more like us, and we share somewhat 'private' personal information on a very limited scale. We see these folk more often and may find time to 'spend' with them in small informal groups or individually now and again.
- Good Friends—The one or two individuals who know our backgrounds, our interests, and at least some of our intimate fears, joys, goals. A good friend (if a husband or wife..then usually 'tagged' with a name such as 'soul-mate') requires MUTUAL exposure of the intimate details of each others lives, troubles, sorrows, joys, needs, etc. To maintain the relationship there must be constant communication and investment of tremendous portions of personal time. If the relationship is cut off due to geographic separation these are the relationships where we say upon meeting again even years later 'it's like we were never apart.' A good friend is 'conversational' in approach, cries with you, laughs with you, holds you accountable to standards that you share, provides advice and support as needed in times of trial and success.

As Anglicans we are careful not to assume that we have a completely separate and individual, non-corporate relation directly with God, or his Son, Jesus Christ as some Protestant religions describe. To say another way, we each individually do not practice our own mini-religions separate and apart from the liturgy, structure and teachings of our Church. Given that caveat, we must search for a simple analogy to at least define closeness / distance; complex / simple communication; dependence / independence. Therefore, the following question is used simply as a means for conceptualization.

Using this analogy of 'friend', where does Jesus Christ fit in your life? Again, jot down your thoughts below, (privately if possible). As you progress in your prayer life we will want to 'check' on your developing relationship to God through Jesus Christ. Be honest!

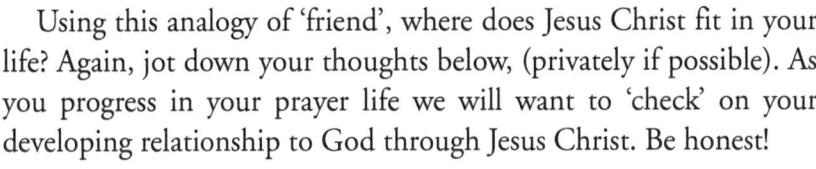

Part of the change that must occur if an intimate relationship is to develop is a change of your image of you, at least in relationship with this intimate person. As I allow the other to be different from my expectations and thus more him self, so, too, I allow myself to be different from my "self" that I love too much and thus become more transparent to him.

When relationships are allowed to develop, more of oneself and that of the other are revealed. Each takes on for the other a life and a personality that is independent of the other's expectations, and in the process each takes on for him a life and personality freed of at least some of the constraints of his own self-image. As they say "get real!" And, in our case, "get real with Jesus Christ!"

If the basis of the relationship, a good friend, is relatively strong, then the unexpected is more readily accepted and accommodated. Thus the need for a deep and abiding trust in God. The difficulty is when an individual has not 'matured' in his/her relationship to the Almighty. You still behave as a child (remember the ridiculous but runaway publication of the 70's *I'm OK, Your OK* giving us PC, PP CC,CP); concerned that your prayers have not been answered, that your requests are not heard, that you must speak ever louder to gain the attention of God through Jesus Christ our Lord!

To move to a mature relationship with our Lord, a relationship that allows prayer as our language of love, we must shed our burdens of sin, our anchors to a denigrating and destructive past; our childish (not child-like) behavior. There is but 'one way' before we can continue in our study and practice of a fruitful "prayer life."

3. Purging of sin—reconciliation to our Lord.

The Eucharist and confession/penance are the principal sources of reconciliation in the Christian life. The sacrament of reconciliation is one of the beautiful gifts that Jesus has given to his church. In fact, it was the very first gift after the resurrection. He breathed on the apostles and said, "Whose sins you shall forgive, they are forgiven." How tremendous that man, ordinary human beings, would have the power to forgive sins in Jesus' name!

For a lot of us that gift of reconciliation is like a Christmas present we opened but didn't appreciate or didn't know what to make of it. So we left it in a closet to gather dust. Some Anglicans seem to experience a certain frustration with a perceived limited effectiveness of regular, corporate confession. The penitent generally feels a sincere repentance, but also hopes to experience a radical change in his or her life, and not only a sense of being pardoned. This is not always the case. In reality, what is lacking on the part of the penitent is a full understanding and appreciation of the complete power of the sacrament, the power that brings the penitent to a HEALING or liberation from the causes of the sins.

These expected results of reconciliation would be better attained if the penitent would approach the sacrament with a defined anticipation of the results, and with the sense of security that the Holy Spirit WILL change the life of the penitent. More explicitly, they ought to expect that a sincere repentance will lead to a more profound union with God and neighbor through the power of the Holy Spirit; so that wounds caused by sins may be healed; that the penitent may be freed from the forces of evil; and that his or her capacity to do good and avoid evil will be strengthened. Screwtape would certainly be desirous of your not experiencing the fruits of confession and reconciliation. All necessary time must be given to the celebration of this sacrament in order to enable the penitent to be sufficiently open, and with confidence in the priest both in corporate and/or private confession, to sincerely expect and receive the desired results.

Experience has shown that those priests and penitents who have given special attention to the celebration of this sacrament have come to appreciate the sacrament as a real and effective gift of God rather than a burden that is better abandoned.

Scriptural Roots

The New Testament is full of instances in which Jesus is forgiving the sins of men and women, and it was just such cases of forgiving which the Pharisees found blasphemous, but which would become for Christians indications of Christ's divinity. Some of the most memorable and beloved stories from Scripture recount the forgiveness of sinners: The Prodigal Son, The Woman caught in adultery, The Thief on the Cross, Peter After his Betrayal Of Jesus. The ministry of forgiveness was controversial because forgiveness was understood as the prerogative of God alone, and because it extended to everyone, every sin without exception.

These stories of forgiveness are not without pattern and rule and very often are associated with healing. In every account that we have, forgiveness is granted to an individual. Jesus forgives and heals particular people, not generic classes of gathered crowds. *Each of these encounters is personal and intimate regardless of whether the confession is done corporately or privately.* A most intimate moment was spent when Jesus spoke to the adulterous woman who had been publicly humiliated; a most personal giving of forgiveness was given to Peter who had three times denied Jesus and was privileged to affirm his love for Him three times. In each instance there is an admission of sin. There is always a change effected by the forgiveness. And there is always an audible proclamation of the forgiveness by Jesus.

Why Confession Today?

If we are honest with ourselves, we must admit that encountering Jesus in the midst of sin and forgiveness remains just as necessary today as it was in the first century time of Christ. We know ourselves as sinners, we cannot escape the waywardness and fickleness of our loves and commitments, the pettiness of our jealousies, and uncontrollable appetites of our passions and desires, our neglect of the poor and needy, our desire to get ahead, even at the cost of other people, our lies, our injustices etc. All of us long for that healing and freedom from guilt offered by Jesus.

But if we grant the necessity of forgiveness, how does that imply the necessity of private as opposed to corporate Confession? Why not apply to Jesus directly in the depths of our heart? Cannot 'individual' confession to Jesus alone in the corporate setting of the Mass suffice to comply with the Scriptural pattern of an individual, personal, admission of sins and proclamation of forgiveness accompanied by a genuine change of life?

YES! If we make of the Scriptural pattern of Jesus' forgiveness of sins a rule, then 'individual' confession in the heart in the corporate setting of the Mass would certainly fulfill the requirements of the law. Yet that pattern of forgiveness demonstrated in Scripture was meant less as a law than as an outline of the real encounter which took place between TWO PEOPLE. We cannot escape the fact that the Jesus who offered forgiveness was a man, present, real, frequently touching the sinner, speaking with a particular accent and inflection. There was nothing particularly inward or "within the heart" about those encounters. It is true that the Jewish people had long experienced forgiveness of sins "in the heart" through sacrificial offerings in the Temple and the Day of Atonement. What was radically different about Jesus' encounter with sinners was that it was FLESH AND BLOOD offering forgiveness to FLESH AND BLOOD. Jesus' offer of forgiveness was a reaffirmation of His earlier solidarity with the human race in His birth. The God who loved us so much as to love us in forgiveness as one of us, and we can only love and be loved as flesh and blood. Thus both private confession "to a priest" and 'individual' confession "in the heart" within the corporate setting of the Mass are both appropriate and acceptable. The practice of confession "to a priest" becomes very important to you if you find that prayer, the love language of our Lord, is blocked by your sins and that corporate confession and absolution somehow does not lift that burden from your shoulders. In any case, you cannot participate fully in the "life" of Christ unless and until you are able to participate fully in a life of prayer—obtaining a release from your sins that block an effective prayer life.

Roots of our present form of confession/reconciliation.

The root of the Anglican form of sacramental forgiveness is the radical notion that everything that God does for us is done as one of us, and as we need to have it done in order that we might believe that it was done. God does not ask us to experience Sacramental forgiveness because it is the only way God forgives, but rather because it is the most fully human way we can know that God forgives us. Experience has aptly shown that in a person there exists a necessity for confession. Psychiatrists, counselors and others in the helping professions very often refer their patients/clients to their ministers, especially priests, because in the matter of sin and guilt, they often feel that it is not within their competency. Somehow human beings know that "in the heart" forgiveness is not sufficient when burdens are terrible and crushing; when prayer seems foreign, confusing, unknown.

The pattern and experience of flesh and blood forgiveness demonstrated by Jesus was continued by Him in His extension to the Church of the power to forgive sins. In Matthew 16:13-23, Jesus gives to Peter and the Church the "Power of the Keys," the power and responsibility to forgive sins. Also in Luke 24:36-49 the Risen Jesus commands the disciples to preach the repentance and forgiveness of sins.

Even St. John the Baptist (the messenger who was sent to prepare the way of the Lord) was asking people to repent and confess: "Then Jerusalem, all Judea, and all the region around the Jordan went out to him and were baptized by him in the Jordan, confessing their sins" [Matthew 3:5]. During the early days of Christianity, the Book of Acts tells us about the many Christians who "had believed" and "came confessing and telling their deeds" (Acts 19:18). So in the early church confession was made publicly and penance conducted publicly for extended periods of months or even years!

We find in the history of this sacrament an early tradition of confession as healing and therapy as well as forgiveness. This gave the priest the role of "doctor of souls" and spiritual doctor for healing wounds caused by sins. This practice became prevalent in the early sixth century when sinners sought out "holy men" as spiritual directors, generally monks, but not necessarily priests. With the arrival of the Irish monks on the continent, the Sacrament was regularly extended to all sin, and became a frequent practice for most people. Some abuses arose from this period, and have extended even to our own day. The notion that forgotten sins are not forgiven, that you must list precisely how many times a sin was committed, that you must promise never to do the sin again, are exaggerations and have never been part of the doctrine of the sacrament. The revision of the Rite or ritual of the sacrament helps to dispel false notions concerning the sacrament.

The Seal of Confession

The seal or secrecy of the sacrament is absolute: It can never be violated for any reason except with the express permission of the one confessing. This means that anything the priest hears in private confession, and anything an interpreter hears or a bystander hears by accident, can never be repeated or acted upon. To break the seal of confession is so serious that it should cause the official deposing of the priest and threatens the very soul of the priest involved.

Other Considerations

The effects of Reconciliation are to resolve the sinners' separation from God and effects of spiritual death, and to restore one to full life with God and the Church. In the Celtic sense this means that the sacrament allows the Trinity to dwell within one's soul, the fullness of God's grace to operate in one's life, and to heal the Mystical Body of Christ, which is all the brothers and sisters of the Lord together as one. It also intended to heal the wounds caused by sin in the sinner and in those offended by the sinner.

To make an examination of conscience, you should:

- Begin with a prayer asking for God's help.
- Review your life
- Tell God you are truly sorry for your sins.
- Make a firm resolution
- Try intently not to sin again.

> Take a moment to ponder the material you just read.
> If you find that it was a bit confusing or that a few points
> Need to be clarified, go back and re-read the section.
>
> If you continue to find confusion or concern, STOP.
>
> Contact a member of the clergy and discuss your concerns or confusion.
> This is a critical time in your prayer life. It is through the Sacrament, Holy Absolution or Penance, that you will find the language of prayer—not as you knew it before, but as a new, loving language of Faith that will slowly become a part of your everyday,
> all day existence in God's creation.

> If you believe that you are ready,
> your next step is to participate with the leader
> of your prayer retreat [if applicable] in the penitents Mass
> that will allow for the following specific prayers
> with sufficient time allotted to accomplish your critical task.

The Sacrament of Holy Absolution or Penance

Prayer Before Reception. Supreme and adorable majesty, God of heaven and earth, I firmly believe You are ever present, and that You see me and know the disposition of my heart. I adore You, and render to You my humble homage, acknowledging You for my God, my Creator, my Sovereign Redeemer. In testimony of this, my faith, I prostrate soul and body before the throne of Your infinite majesty, and offer You the adoration that is due to You alone. O Father of light, who enlightens everyone who comes into the world, send into my heart a ray of light, of love, of sorrow, that I may know, detest, confess the sins I have committed against You. I wish to see my sins in their entire enormity, just as they are in Your sight. I wish to detest them for my love of You, and to confess them with the same sincerity now that I would give at the moment of death. I know, my God, that this knowledge of my sins, the sorrow for them, the sincerity in declaring them to your minister can come only from Your bounty. As You wish that the sinner should not die, You sent Your Son into the world to purchase his forgiveness, I implore this grace through the merits of Jesus Christ, who died upon the cross of my sins, and who is now sitting at Your right hand, where He continually shows You, in my behalf, the wounds He endured for me.

Holy angels and all the Saints, who has been a spectator to all my crimes, help me discover the sins that I have committed against our God. Pray for me that I may bring forth fruits of penance. Amen.

Offering of the Examination of Conscience Jesus, my God and Saviour, I offer You the examination that I will make, that Your divine justice may be glorified in it. I look to You with confidence for the grace to do it well. In the spirit of charity, to please You, and to accomplish Your holy will, together with every intention that can procure You the greatest honor and glory, I undertake this examination. (*A sincere examination of conscience will now take place.*)

Act of a Contrite Heart—Confession ALMIGHTY God, Father of our Lord Jesus Christ, Maker of all things, Judge of all men; We acknowledge and bewail our manifold sins and wickedness, Which we, from time to time, most grievously have committed, By thought, word, and deed, Against thy Divine Majesty, Provoking most justly thy wrath and indignation against us. We do earnestly repent, And are heartily sorry for these our misdoings; The remembrance of them is grievous unto us; The burden of them is intolerable. Have mercy upon us, Have mercy upon us, most merciful Father; For thy Son our Lord Jesus Christ's sake, Forgive us all that is past; And grant that we may ever hereafter Serve and please thee In newness of life, To the honour and glory of thy Name; Through Jesus Christ our Lord. Amen. (BCP, 1928)

Prayer After Reception My dearest Jesus, I have told all my sins to the best of my ability. I have sincerely tried to make a good confession and I know that you have forgiven me. Thank you dear Jesus! Your divine heart is full of love and mercy for poor sinners. I love you dear Jesus; you are so good to me. My loving Savior, I shall try to keep from sin and to love you more each day.

Part Three:

Types of Prayer and Their Proper Exercise

Let's Talk About Prayer

The ancient Celtic Church was at ease with formal prayer; they kept the Offices in their communities. But we also have many records of more spontaneous prayers. Prayer was often quite physical. People would pray as they walked. Crossing yourself was a regular part of prayer, as was the drawing of an imaginary circle around you in one of the encircling prayers. Celtic Christians found it as natural to pray during the milking of a cow, as they did in church—and they still do! In this way the Celtic Church was returning to Jewish roots, for in Jewish spirituality there has always been a strong earthiness in prayer. In the same fashion Celtic prayer was always deeply Trinitarian. Coming into the presence of God in prayer meant coming into the presence of all three members of the Trinity.

Thus, we might say that the types or styles of prayer have an Anglican tradition that is quite broad and varied. For example, the Christian family is the first place of education in prayer. Based on the Sacrament of Marriage, the family is the "domestic church" where God's children learn to pray "as the Church" and to persevere in prayer. For young children in particular, daily family prayer is the first witness of the Church's living memory as awakened patiently by the Holy Spirit. This is done first through the morning and evening offices and Prayers of the Family of the Book of Common Prayer (BCP) but also through additional prayers.

Ordained ministers are also responsible for the formation in prayer of their brothers and sisters in Christ. Servants of the Good Shepherd, they are ordained to lead the People of God to the living waters of prayer: the

Word of God, the liturgy, the theological life (the life of faith, hope, and charity), and the God in concrete situations.

Many religious have consecrated their whole lives to prayer. Hermits, monks, and nuns since the time of the desert fathers have devoted their time to praising God and interceding for his people. The consecrated life cannot be sustained or spread without prayer; it is one of the living sources of contemplation and the spiritual life of the Church.

The catechesis of children, young people, and adults aims at teaching them to meditate on The Word of God in personal prayer, practicing it in liturgical prayer, and internalizing it at all times in order to bear fruit in a new life. Catechesis is also a time for the discernment and education of popular piety. The memorization of basic prayers offers an essential support to the life of prayer, but it is important to help learners savor their meaning.

Prayer groups, indeed "schools of prayer," are today one of the signs and one of the driving forces of renewal of prayer in the Church, provided they drink from authentic wellsprings of Christian prayer. Concern for ecclesial communion is a sign of true prayer in the Church.

The Holy Spirit gives to certain of the faithful the gifts of wisdom, faith and discernment for the sake of this common good that is prayer (spiritual direction). Men and women so endowed are true servants of the living tradition of prayer. According to St. John of the Cross, the person wishing to advance toward perfection should take care into whose hands he entrusts himself, for as the master is, so will the disciple be, and as the father is so will be the son. And further: "In addition to being learned and discreet a director should be experienced.... If the spiritual director has no experience of the spiritual life, he will be incapable of leading into it the souls whom God is calling to it, and he will not even understand them."

Now, are there specific places favorable for prayer? The answer is Yes!

The church, the house of God, is the proper place for the liturgical prayer of the parish community. It is also the privileged place for adoration of the mystery of the real presence of Christ in the Blessed Sacrament.

The choice of a favorable place is not a matter of indifference for true prayer.

For personal prayer, this can be a "prayer corner" or "home altar" with the Sacred Scriptures and icons, in order to be there, in secret, before our Father. In a Christian family, this kind of little oratory fosters prayer in common.

In regions where monasteries or retreat houses exist you might consider experiencing the surroundings with a small group from your church or even your extended family. The vocation of these communities is to further the participation of the faithful and to provide necessary solitude for more intense personal prayer.

Pilgrimages evoke our earthly journey toward heaven and are traditionally very special occasions for renewal in prayer. For pilgrims seeking living water, shrines are special places for living the forms of Christian prayer "in Church."

Now, if we were to classify prayer into broad categories, how would we do that? Well, as tradition describes, we could establish rather broad categories or classifications as vocal or mental, private or public.

In vocal prayer some outward action, usually verbal expression, accompanies the internal act implied in every form of prayer. This external action not only helps to keep us attentive to the prayer, but it also adds to its intensity. Examples of it occur in the prayer of the Israelites in captivity (Ex., 2:23); again after their idolatry among the Canaanites (Judges, 3:9); the Lord's Prayer (Matt., 6:9); Christ's own prayer after resuscitating Lazarus (John, 11:41); and the testimonies in (Heb., 5:7, and 8:15). And we must not forget that our hymns, canticles, and other forms of prayer (yes a hymn is not just a song to please us, but a prayer to please our Lord) would not exist except as verbal forms of prayer; it was common in the Church from the beginning; nor has it ever been denied, except by groups like the Wyclifites and the Quietists.

The Wyclifites objected to it as unnecessary, as God does not need our words to know what goes on in our souls, and prayer being a spiritual act need be performed by the soul alone without the body. Not only does this philosophy reject the Jewish tradition of the Christian faith, but it wrongly assumes (as we shall see) that all individuals are capable of mature, meditative prayer—at least in the beginning phases of their prayer journey. The Quietists regarded all external action in prayer as an untoward disturbance or interference with the passivity of the soul required, in their opinion, to pray properly.

In the Anglican tradition prayer must be the action of the entire man—mind, body as well as the spirit; that God who created all three is pleased with the service of all three, and that when the three act in unison they help instead of interfere with one another's activities.

The Wyclifites objected not only to all external expression of prayer generally, but to vocal prayer in its proper sense, viz. prayer expressed in set form of words, excepting only the Our Father. The use of a variety of such forms is sanctioned by the prayer over the first-fruits (Deut., 26:13). If it is right to use one form, that of the Our Father, why not others? The Litany, Collective and Eucharistic prayers of the early Church were surely set forms, and the familiar daily prayers, the Our Father, Hail Mary, Apostles' Creed, Confiteor, all attest the usage of the Church in this respect and the preference of the faithful for such approved forms to others of their own composition.

In the same fashion, postures in prayer are also an evidence of the tendency in human nature to express inward sentiment by outward sign. Not only among Jews and Christians, but among pagan peoples also, certain postures were considered appropriate in prayer, as, for instance, standing with arms raised among the Romans. The postures favored by the early Christians, standing with hands extended, as Christ on the Cross, according to Tertullian; or with hands raised towards heaven, with bowed heads, or, for the faithful, with eyes raised toward heaven, and, for the catechumens, with eyes bent on the earth; prostration, kneeling, genuflection, and such gestures as striking the breast are all outward signs of the reverence proper for prayer, whether in public or private.

Our Anglican heritage does not officially discriminate between any of these postures although the traditional and more devout postures seem to be preferred as evidenced in the rubrics of the BCP. Variations do occur in limited fashion between churches, within the Sanctuary amongst priests, deacons and acolytes. It would be foolish not to anticipate such differences among the laity.

Although we should not make prayer some form of complex, esoteric study of differing styles; we must try to place "all the words" about prayer into some form such that they are understood in somewhat similar fashion and that common sense can come to grips with the multitude of different phrases, names, etc. To make sense of the various types and styles let us try a simple paradigm.

Prayer Style

Informal (colloquial); using a conversational tone without memorized, or written prayers or procedures—the relationship with Jesus is termed 'personal,' or as close friend. Our fundamental and reformed brothers and sisters and others particularly favor this form of prayer.

Formal (ritual): using formal prayers or rites, like the rosary or the Book of Common Prayer (BCP). The relationship with God is more formal, usually with a personal sense of awe for the Creator that maintains a "psychological distance" of sorts, but, when properly understood also fosters a feeling of closeness or warmth under the protection of the Good Shepherd. This is clearly the preference of the major divisions within the One, Holy, Catholic and Apostolic Church.

Prayer Expression

- *Vocal or Quiet*

Prayer Message (somewhat in order of general understanding and complexity):

- *Simple Prayer*
- *Confession or supplication / lamentation*: The repentance of wrongdoing and asking for forgiveness
- *Sacramental or Incarnational*: Prayer of the Church as Liturgy and Eucharist
- *Thanksgiving:* Offering gratitude
- *Adoration and oblation*: Giving honor and praise; offering up gifts to our Lord (daily life, family relationships, work efforts, etc.)
- *Petition*: Asking for something for one's self, possibly with the help of either or both the living and the dead.
- *Intercession:* Asking for something for others. Again, possibly with the help of either or both the living and the dead.
- *Meditation / Contemplation*: A deep, mature communion with our Lord in prayer life. The message is always in 'quiet.'
- *Unceasing Prayer*
- *Covenantal*: Giving of oneself totally to the will of the Triune God

You most certainly may have differing ways of thinking about prayer from those listed above. But, for our tasks here, allow the above listing simply for sake of common understanding within these pages.

In the next several chapters we will review the various prayer methods. Understand that the differences are not simply in the 'names.'

There are substantive differences that determine practice. As such a number of faithful 'pray-ers' in a parish will be at differing levels of prayer method—differing capabilities to properly speak to our Lord. You may experience this difference yourself with such feelings as; "This type of prayer is rather silly" (I am uncomfortable with this) or "Anyone can just sit and 'contemplate' Jesus" (I really don't know the difference between simple communication and a total prayer life)!

Questions in preparation

We will contemplate certain questions toward our preparation for prayer, confession and Holy Communion. Consider each of the following questions and note any issues that exist or remain to some degree in your life relevant to each. Upon such contemplation and confession and receipt of the Holy Eucharist we shall be in the Grace of our Lord and the fruits of prayer shall become available to our lives.

Take some time on each question. This is not a list that you "check off" and take to the grocery store! Each is a direct consideration of your present standing with our Lord and Saviour. Treat each question with reverence; dispose of the question if not relevant to you or contemplate the issue(s) raised by each question such that you may eradicate them from your life through the confessional. If you use this little book during a retreat, then you should discuss any issues raised and noted below with the priest-in-charge of the retreat. If you read this text alone then you should discuss any issues with your parish priest or another individual who serves as your prayer partner (anamchara) or a member of your payer group; accountability for the resolution / confession of issues is paramount in your journey at this time.

Take a pencil and write that which comes to mind just below each question.

- How conscious am I of the real goal of my life? Of the discipline needed to achieve it?

- Do I consider that I have been living for the Lord?

- How aware am I of the grace of God that has called me to my station in life?

- How operative has the gospel been in my everyday life?

- Do I ever reflect on what the "commitment of faith" should mean in my life?

- How often do I ever seek to find the traces of God's activity in the world about me?

- How often do I reflect on the Divine Judgment?

- Do I truly listen to my conscience?

- Do I truly feel that God's law is written on my heart?

- Is my heart truly open to others and contrite in spirit?

- Does my faith measure up to what God expects of me as a Christian, and a Christian in prayer for myself and for others?

- Do I realize what such a commitment of faith should mean in my own conduct, especially in my dealings with others?

- How vital is my faith in the risen Christ and how concretely does my conduct of life amount to a service of him as Lord?

- Am I ready to labor with the Lord in this ministry of prayer and follow him in suffering or pain, so that I might also come to follow him to glory?

- Do I feel summoned in His grace?

- Do I truly know both my Adamic condition of sinful heritage and the immense gift of uprightness that has come to me in Christ Jesus?

- Do I allow the identification with Christ to surface to my consciousness, to the level of my conscious activity, my prayers?

- How conscious am I of the influence of the indwelling Holy Spirit in my life and activity?

- Do I really want to be led more by Christ's Spirit?

- Is my zeal for God rightly informed and motivated?

- Do I resist the call of God?

- How aware am I of living my Christian life as an act of worship of God?

- How can I learn to respect the conscience of others?

Take time to review any issues that you listed above with your priest-in-charge of your prayer retreat, your parish priest or your anamchara. Your considerations should be to increase your capabilities to be with our Lord in all your thoughts and actions. Explore a personal plan that will enhance these existing strengths or correct any deficiencies such that prayer becomes that much more powerful through the presence of the Holy Spirit in your heart. Think carefully and jot down no less than three and no more than five "targets-of-success" that you will address personally within the next six months AND *for which you will be held accountable.* Keep your targets short, to the point, and in His guidance for your life.

1.

2.

3.

4.

5.

Once your charge concerning the above questions is complete, you are ready to continue in your journey of prayer—read on!

Simple Prayer

Many times we avoid "prayer" as we vaguely perceive it. Our problem is that we assume prayer is always something to master the way we master algebra or auto mechanics. That puts us in the "on-top" position, where we are competent and in control. But when praying, we come "underneath," where we calmly and deliberately surrender control and become incompetent. We will learn this more intently later as we discuss meditative / contemplative prayer.

The truth of the matter is, we all come to prayer with all types of motives—altruistic and selfish, merciful and hateful, loving and bitter. Don't allow this to scare you away from the arms of our Lord. *We will never unravel the good from the bad, the pure from the impure until we join our Lord in heaven.* We do not have to be perfect to enter into the bond of prayer…that is why we are saved by grace…we live by it…we must pray with it.

God receives us just as we are; and our prayers just as they are.

In simple prayer we bring ourselves before God just as we are. Like children before a loving father, we open our hearts and make our request. We are the focus of the simple prayer. Although we are flawed, we fail time and again and request forgiveness time and again, we must pray time and again; maintain our loving relationship with our dear God. Such simple prayers are the most common in Scripture (Exodus 32:32, 2 Kings 4:16, Psalms 119:97). Abraham, Joseph, Joshua, Hannah, David, Gideon, Ruth, Peter, James, John are in your company.

Simple prayer involves ordinary people bringing ordinary concerns to a loving and compassionate father. There is no pretense. You do not need to list your pure or saintly actions or thoughts…they are of no importance to your prayer….your Father knew of them before you.

Simple prayer is not the only way to pray but it is the foundation for all other prayer. We must understand and accept that, as sophisticated as we would like to be, we will always return to the "childlike" (not childish) simple prayers with our loving God.

In simple prayer we should feel free to "pace the floor" with God in the Jewish tradition, share how we feel, discuss our hurts and our hates, ask the question "why me?" or "why my child?" By sharing such human concerns we are asking our Lord to heal that which we cannot see, that which we do not understand. At this stage it is OK to vehemently ask…"Why?"

This is very much akin to the discovery of God in the daily and the ordinary, not in the spectacular and the heroic. As with our Lord Jesus Christ, prayer and a relationship with God the Father should be in every action, in all occupations (including being a carpenter or a rabbi) in all actions taken. All actions, all jobs and, in particular, the lowliest of tasks are highly valued in the order of the kingdom of God as a sweet smelling incense wafting to the heavens. "The message about Christ's death on the cross is nonsense to those who are being lost: but for us who are being saved it is God's power." (1Cor 1:18)

Slowly and thoughtfully make the sign of the cross, upon yourself. Say the words from the baptismal service.

I sign with the sign of the Cross, in token that hereafter I shall not be ashamed to confess the faith of Christ crucified, and to fight under his banner, against sin, the world, and the devil; and to continue Christ's faithful soldier and servant unto life's end.

Use this as a means of turning in to, becoming aware of, the great love of God towards you. Let the cross be a sign of your deliverance, your freedom.

Contemplate, now, allowing the saving power of God to be at work in your life

- Let His power come into your weakness
- Let His love come to your loneliness
- Let His hope dispel your fears
- Let His peace bring calm to your troubles
- Let His Spirit come into your heart to conquer darkness and spark your Faith

Pray the following Celtic prayer:
> *Blessed Three,*
> *I come in humility,*
> *I come by grace,*
> *I come with confidence,*
> *I pray in your name,*
> *Father, Son, and Holy Spirit*
>   (General prayers attributed to St. Aidan of Lindesfarne)

Prayers of Confession or Supplication

This is the very first prayer, beyond simple prayer, that we must understand and perform. As Christ used this prayer to prepare for all that was to come, so we must do the same: "And he went a little further, and fell on his face, and prayed, saying, O my Father, if it be possible, let this cup pass from me: nevertheless not as I will, but as thou wilt." (Matt 26:39). The Psalmist also knew this necessity prior to prayers of praise and thanksgiving: "But be not thou far from me, O LORD: O my strength, haste thee to help me. Deliver my soul from the sword; my darling from the power of the dog. Save me from the lion's mouth: for thou hast heard me from the horns of the unicorns." (Ps 22:19-21). This is the prayer of the Sacrament of Absolution or Confession.

As in the Psalms, we must move through lamentations to understand, extol, praise our Lord as we recover from our past and enter our new prayer life.

Times of seeming desertion and absence and abandonment appear to be universal among those who have walked this path of faith before us...sooner or later, we too will feel forsaken by God. Known as *Deus Absconditus*—the God who is hidden. We do everything possible; pray (although we know that it is stale), do good works; worship each Sabbath, attend Morning Prayer, attend mid-week Eucharist...but, nothing! This is truly an experience of spiritual desolation....being lost in the desert.

We question. We doubt. We struggle. Nothing seems to help. Our words, as faithful as we may desire to be at the moment, seem empty, lifeless, and useless. (Psalms 22:2, 42:9). Finally, we wonder not where God may be in our trials, but whether there is a God at all. Such feelings have variously been called "the dark night of the soul," "the cloud of unknowing," "the dark night of faith."

But you are not left behind. This is a part of prayer; a part of the journey that we as mankind, in our frailties and limited understandings, must follow. It will come. It is a part of our prayer experience.

There are times when we "hear" our Lord say wait, wait and be silent. At these times He may also be silent—silent for months on end. But we must trust our Lord. He understands our needs better that we do. He places us in a period of silence, The Purifying Silence. Saint John of the Cross speaks of two such purifications that can occur to each of us in these situations.

The first involves stripping us of dependence upon exterior results. We loose our attachments to externalities, we begin to slowly loose control to a greater and spiritual power. We find that once we are no longer dependent upon externalities we come to understand that we cannot control our Lord…it is His will that is to be done.

The second involves stripping us of dependence upon interior results. We begin to question the very foundation of life in the Spirit. God allows us to move to the brink of the chasm, to see the depth to which one might fall and be consumed by darkness. All distractions are gone; we are focused. All to rebuild our Faith, to shake us from our own self-deception, to remind us that both evil and good do exist and Faith is that highway away from spiritual death and back to our Lord. We regain our capacity for patience, humility, and heart-felt love. And our grandest lesson; *trust precedes a true Faith*.

The message is covered in an earlier section of this text (The Sacrament of Holy Absolution or Penance) and is used in preparation for all other prayers addressed.

Sacramental or Incarnational Prayer

Although formal and informal techniques of prayer are both wonderful and God-sanctioned, we as Anglicans are those who generally prefer more formal prayer. For us the regular patterns of devotion form a kind of skeletal structure upon which we can build the muscle and tissue of unceasing prayer. Never fear…these regular patterns called rituals are, in fact, God ordained means of grace. The Old Testament and Psalms are rich with such rituals, instruction and repetitive prayers.

There are many freedoms provided by liturgical prayer. Such formal prayers;

- Help us articulate the yearnings of the heart that cry for expression
- Help us unite with the "communion of saints." This is far greater than our singular prayer to the Lord. We join the voices of the faithful who existed over a period of millennia. Your prayer joins St. Augustine, Iranaeus, St. Jerome and others!!
- Help us stand against the temptation to be spectacular and entertaining. Increasingly the words focus more and more on God and less and less on ourselves
- Help us to resist the temptation of private religion, letting our petty concerns be the whole burden of our prayer. We are brought back to community, to the teachings of the church, to sound doctrine.

- Help us avoid the familiarity that breeds contempt; the formality of the liturgy help us realize that we are in the presence of real Royalty.

Even so, it us understandable that concerns exist in the mind of the pray-er:

- What you are doing is rote. You are not really thinking about what you are praying. *But this is an asset not a liability.* I am free to enter into the depth of my need rather than describing my need.
- The words you are using are archaic…how can they be relevant. Again, an asset. More often the argument for relevancy is simply a temptation of the devil that needs to be resisted. *Liturgies conserve the best of tradition and avoid mindless fads.* The Divinely inspired words will never be archaic…Satan simply wants us to believe this to be so.
- The words are a vain repetition that Jesus asks us to avoid. But is a crude, colloquial language equal to spiritual and no others? Certainly a possible idolatry as is cautioned of the liturgical finesse. "But when ye pray, use not vain repetitions, as the heathen do: for they think that they shall be heard for their much speaking." (Matt 6:7). But, then a "set" liturgical prayer is recommended, that which we all accept!

"After this manner therefore pray ye: Our Father which art in heaven, Hallowed be thy name. Thy kingdom come. Thy will be done in earth, as it is in heaven. Give us this day our daily bread. And forgive us our debts, as we forgive our debtors. And lead us not into temptation, but deliver us from evil: For thine is the kingdom, and the power, and the glory, for ever. Amen." (Matt 6:9-13)

Thus it is both 'unguided colloquial prayer' as well as a shallow understanding of the beauty of the liturgy that should be avoided.

The Gospels tell us that Christ prayed the way a devout Jew faithful to the law prayed. Just as he made pilgrimages to Jerusalem at the prescribed times with his parents as a child, so he later journeyed to the temple there with his disciples to celebrate the high feasts. Surely he sang with holy enthusiasm along with his people the exultant hymns in which the pilgrim's joyous anticipation streamed forth: "I rejoiced when I heard them say: Let us go to God's house." (Ps 122:1) From his last supper with his disciples, we know that Jesus said the old blessing over bread, wine, and the fruits of the earth, as they are prayed to this day. So he fulfilled one of the most sacred religious duties: the ceremonial Passover Seder to commemorate deliverance from slavery in Egypt. And perhaps this very gathering gives us the profoundest glimpse into Christ's prayer and the key to understanding the prayer of the Church.

While they were at supper, Jesus took bread, broke the bread, and gave it to his disciples, saying, "Take eat, this is my body which is given for you; Do this in remembrance of me."

In the same way, he took the cup, filled with wine. He gave thanks, giving the cup to his disciples, saying, "Drink ye all of this; for this is my Blood of the New Testament, which is shed for you, and for many, for the remission of sins; Do this, as oft as ye shall drink it, in remembrance of me."

Blessing and distributing bread and wine were part of the Passover rite. But here both receive an entirely new meaning. This is where the life of the Church begins. Through the Word of Christ, the old blessings become life-giving words. Visible creation, which he entered when he became a human being, is now united with him in a new, mysterious way. The Word's life-giving power is bound to the sacrifice.

In place of Solomon's temple, Christ has built a temple of living stones, the communion of saints. At its center, he stands as the eternal high priest;

on its altar he is himself the perpetual sacrifice. And, in turn, the whole of creation is drawn into the "liturgy," the ceremonial worship service: the fruits of the earth as the mysterious offerings, the flowers and the lighted candlesticks, the carpets and the curtain, the ordained priest, and the anointing and blessing of God's house.

The liturgical unity of the heavenly with the earthly church, both of which thank God "through Christ," finds its most powerful expression in the preface and the Sanctus of the Mass. However, the liturgy leaves no doubt that we are not yet full citizens of the heavenly Jerusalem, but pilgrims on the way to our eternal home. We must always prepare ourselves before we may dare to lift our eyes to the luminous heights and to unite our voices with the "holy, holy, holy" of the heavenly chorus. Each created thing to be used in the worship service must be withdrawn from its profane use, must be purified and consecrated. Before the priest climbs the steps to the altar, he must cleanse himself by acknowledging his sins, and the faithful must do so with him. Prior to each step as the offertory continues, he must repeat his plea for the forgiveness of sins for himself and for those gathered around him as well as for all to whom the fruits of the sacrifice are to flow. The sacrifice itself is a sacrifice of expiation that transforms the faithful as it transforms the gifts, unlocks heaven for them, and enables them to sing a hymn of praise pleasing to God. All that we need to be received into the communion of saints is summed up in the seven petitions of the Our Father, which the Lord did not pray in his own name, but to instruct us. We say it before communion, and when we say it sincerely and from our hearts and receive communion in the proper spirit, it fulfills all of our petitions. Communion delivers us from evil, because it cleanses us of forgiveness of past sins and strengthens us in the face of temptations. It is itself the bread of life that we need daily to grow into eternal life.

So we see again how the offertory, communion, and the praise of God are internally related. Participation in the sacrifice and in the sacrificial meal actually transforms the soul into a living stone in the city of God in fact, each individual soul into a temple of God. (Edith Stein, *The Hidden Life*)

In the New Covenant, prayer is the living relationship of the children of God with their Father who is good beyond measure, with his Son Jesus Christ and with the Holy Sprit. The grace of the Kingdom is "the union of the entire holy and royal Trinity..with the whole human spirit." (St. Gregory of Nazinzus) Thus, the life of prayer is the habit of being in the presence of the thrice-holy God and in communion with Him. This communion of life is always possible because, through Baptism, we have already been united with Christ, "For if we have been planted together in the likeness of his death, we shall be also in the likeness of his resurrection:" (Rom 6:5)

Prayers of Thanksgiving

We are taught early in life to be grateful and to thank one another for gifts or efforts on our behalf. In the same way we thank the Communion of Saints for supporting us by their fellowship "of love and prayer" and surrounding us "by their witness to God's power and mercy." Most important of all we give thanks to Jesus Christ and the Triune God, the Giver of all good things.

The Prayer of Thanksgiving characterizes the prayer of the Church that, in celebrating the Eucharist (Thanksgiving), reveals and becomes more fully what she is. Jesus set us free from sin and death. Indeed, St. Paul tells us Jesus has reconciled everything in His Person, both in the Heavens and on earth, making peace through the Blood of His Cross. He has renewed all things. We the members of the Mystical Body participate in the thanksgiving of Jesus our Head. "As in the prayer of petition, every event and need can become an offering of thanksgiving." St. Paul tells us to dedicate ourselves to thanksgiving. His letters often begin and end with thanksgiving.

I believe that gratitude is very important to God. Look at the story of the ten lepers who were cured by Jesus. Only one returned to offer thanksgiving. What was Jesus' reaction? We are told that Jesus, on more than one occasion, lifted His eyes to Heaven giving thanks. He also specifically thanked His Father in Heaven.

As in the prayer of petition, every event and need can become an offering of thanksgiving. The letters of St. Paul often begin and end with thanksgiving, and the Lord Jesus is always present in it: "In every thing give thanks: for this is the will of God in Christ Jesus concerning you." (1Thes 5:18); "Continue in prayer, and watch in the same with thanksgiving;" (Col 4:2) "Be careful for nothing; but in every thing by prayer and supplication with thanksgiving let your requests be made known unto God." (Phil 4:6) "First, I thank my God through Jesus Christ for you all, that your faith is spoken of throughout the whole world." (Rom 1:8). "Giving thanks always for all things unto God and the Father in the name of our Lord Jesus Christ;" (Eph 5:20)

In thanksgiving we give glory to God for what he has done for us; in praise we give glory to God for who he is in himself. The Psalter is replete with statements of thanksgiving. "I will give thee thanks in the great congregation: I will praise thee among much people." (Ps 106:1). "Praise ye the LORD. O give thanks unto the LORD; for he is good: for his mercy endureth for ever" (Ps 35:18). "I will praise thee, O LORD, with my whole heart; I will shew forth all thy marvelous works." (Ps 9:1)

Prayers of Adoration, Praise and Oblation

In both the Hebrew of the Old Testament and the Greek of the New, the word for 'praise' can also be translated as 'honor.' When we acknowledge someone for an accomplishment we honor him or her. Each of us has our own heroes, whether friends, sports figures, statesmen, or churchmen. St. Peter commands us to honor all the saints (1Peter 2:17). Since we have no power in ourselves to help ourselves, by honoring our Church's heroes we honor God. Ultimately, it is God's very being that draws our praise. This type of prayer is often called *arrow prayer* or *ejaculatory prayer* because of their briefness and spontaneity.

Adoration is an attitude on our part that acknowledges that we are creatures before God our Creator. We exalt God's greatness because He made us and He sets us free from evil.

With adoration we render homage in the spirit to the "King of Glory." It is a respectful silence in the presence of the awesome God. We adore the thrice-holy and sovereign God of love. Some have had a glimpse into this mystery. The children of Fatima, Portugal come to my mind. When an angel appeared to them in 1916 he invited them to pray with him. The angel knelt and bowed his forehead to the ground praying three times, "My God, I believe, I ADORE, I hope and I love You…" After the angel departed, these children felt so immersed in the presence of God that they were unable to speak for the rest of the day. The second time the angel came he again prostrate himself and this time prayed three times, "Most Holy Trinity, Father, Son and Holy Spirit, I ADORE You profoundly…" The children described their experience as one of feeling "lost in God." God's love and His very being are overwhelming to His creatures. In the Old Testament those who "saw" God were amazed that they were still alive. But even we who have not seen God can be awestruck when we think about all He has created. Just look at the stars some night!

Adoration, then, is the spontaneous yearning of the heart to worship, honor, magnify, and bless God. This is the prayer of selfless devotion. We ask for nothing but to cherish him. "To the end that my glory may sing praise to thee, and not be silent. O LORD my God, I will give thanks unto thee for ever." (Ps 30:12).

David appointed special singers to do nothing but praise the Lord before the Ark of the Covenant. "And he appointed certain of the Levites to minister before the ark of the LORD, and to record, and to thank and praise the LORD God of Israel: Asaph the chief, and next to him Zechariah, Jeiel, and Shemiramoth, and Jehiel, and Mattithiah, and Eliab, and Benaiah, and Obededom: and Jeiel with psalteries and with harps; but Asaph made a sound with cymbals; Benaiah also and Jahaziel the priests with trumpets continually before the ark of the covenant of God."

Then on that day David delivered first this psalm to thank the LORD into the hand of Asaph and his brethren.

> "Give thanks unto the LORD, call upon his name, make known his deeds among the people. Sing unto him, sing psalms unto him, talk ye of all his wondrous works. Glory ye in his holy name: let the heart of them rejoice that seek the LORD. Seek the LORD and his strength, seek his face continually. Remember his marvellous works that he hath done, his wonders, and the judgments of his mouth; O ye seed of Israel his servant, ye children of Jacob, his chosen ones. He is the LORD our God; his judgments are in all the earth. Be ye

mindful always of his covenant; the word which he commanded to a thousand generations; Even of the covenant which he made with Abraham, and of his oath unto Isaac; And hath confirmed the same to Jacob for a law, and to Israel for an everlasting covenant, Saying, Unto thee will I give the land of Canaan, the lot of your inheritance; When ye were but few, even a few, and strangers in it. And when they went from nation to nation, and from one kingdom to another people; He suffered no man to do them wrong: yea, he reproved kings for their sakes, Saying, Touch not mine anointed, and do my prophets no harm. Sing unto the LORD, all the earth; shew forth from day to day his salvation. Declare his glory among the heathen; his marvellous works among all nations. For great is the LORD, and greatly to be praised: he also is to be feared above all gods. For all the gods of the people are idols: but the LORD made the heavens. Glory and honour are in his presence; strength and gladness are in his place. Give unto the LORD, ye kindreds of the people, give unto the LORD glory and strength. Give unto the LORD the glory due unto his name: bring an offering, and come before him: worship the LORD in the beauty of holiness. Fear before him, all the earth: the world also shall be stable, that it be not moved. Let the heavens be glad, and let the earth rejoice: and let men say among the nations, The LORD reigneth. Let the sea roar, and the fulness thereof: let the fields rejoice, and all that is therein. Then shall the trees of the wood sing out at the presence of the LORD, because he cometh to judge the earth. O give thanks unto the LORD; for he is good; for his mercy endureth for ever. And say ye, Save us, O God of our salvation, and gather us together, and deliver us from the heathen, that we may give thanks to thy holy name, and glory in thy praise. Blessed be the

LORD God of Israel for ever and ever. And all the people said, Amen, and praised the LORD." (1 Cor 16:4-36)

But praise is certainly greater than the prayer of thanksgiving as previously discussed, as thanksgiving still involves ourselves to some degree where praise is selfless, it is focused on our Lord and Saviour and provides the type of prayer of adoration of the angels. "Praise ye the LORD. Praise the LORD, O my soul. While I live will I praise the LORD: I will sing praises unto my God while I have any being." (Ps 146:1-2). "I will bless the LORD at all times: his praise shall continually be in my mouth. My soul shall make her boast in the LORD: the humble shall hear thereof, and be glad. O magnify the LORD with me, and let us exalt his name together." (Ps 34:1-3) "Ye that fear the LORD, praise him; all ye the seed of Jacob, glorify him; and fear him, all ye the seed of Israel." (Ps 22:23). "And he hath put a new song in my mouth, even praise unto our God: many shall see it, and fear, and shall trust in the LORD." (Ps 40:3) "Enter into his gates with thanksgiving, and into his courts with praise: be thankful unto him, and bless his name." (Ps 100:4)

Also the writer of Hebrews states "By him therefore let us offer the sacrifice of praise to God continually, that is, the fruit of our lips giving thanks to his name." (Heb 13:15)

And the writer of Revelations tells us that praise is a serious matter. "And I beheld, and I heard the voice of many angels round about the throne and the beasts and the elders: and the number of them was ten thousand times ten thousand, and thousands of thousands; Saying with a loud voice, Worthy is the Lamb that was slain to receive power, and riches, and wisdom, and strength, and honour, and glory, and blessing. And every creature which is in heaven, and on the earth, and under the earth, and such as are in the sea, and all that are in them, heard I saying, Blessing, and honour, and glory, and power, be unto him that sitteth upon the throne, and unto the Lamb for ever and ever. And the four beasts said, Amen. And the four and twenty elders fell down and worshipped him that liveth for ever and ever." (Rev 5:11-14)

Praise is the form of prayer that recognizes immediately that God is God. It lauds God for his own sake and gives him glory, quite beyond what he does, but simply because HE IS. It shares in the blessed happiness of the pure of heart who love God in faith before seeing him in glory. By praise, the Spirit is joined to our spirits to bear witness that we are children of God, testifying to the only Son in whom we are adopted and by whom we glorify the Father. "The Spirit itself beareth witness with our spirit, that we are the children of God:" (Rom 8:16) Praise embraces the other forms of prayer and carries them toward him who is its source and goal: "But to us there is but one God, the Father, of whom are all things, and we in him; and one Lord Jesus Christ, by whom are all things, and we by him." (1Cor 8:6).

St. Luke in his gospel often expresses wonder and praise at the marvels of Christ and in his Acts of the Apostles stresses them as actions of the Holy Spirit: the community of Jerusalem, the invalid healed by Peter and John, the crowd that gives glory to God for that, and the pagans of Pisidia who "were glad and glorified the word of God." (Acts 13:48).

"Speaking to yourselves in psalms and hymns and spiritual songs, singing and making melody in your heart to the Lord;" (Eph 5:19) Like the inspired writers of the New Testament, the first Christian communities read the Book of Psalms in a new way, seeing in it the mystery of Christ. In the newness of the Spirit, they also composed hymns and canticles in the light of the unheard-of event that God accomplished in his Son: his Incarnation, his death which conquered death, his Resurrection, and Ascension to the right hand of the Father (Phil 2:6-11; Col 1:15-20; Eph 5:14; 1Tim 3:16, 6:15-16; 2Tim 2:11-13) Doxology, the praise of God, arises from this "marvelous work" of the whole economy of salvation. (Eph 1:3-14; Rom 16:25-27; Eph 3:20,21; Jude 24:25)

The Revelation of "what must soon take place," the Apocalypse, is borne along by the songs of the heavenly liturgy but also by the intercession of the "witnesses" (martyrs). "And in her was found the blood of prophets, and of saints, and of all that were slain upon the earth. And after these things I heard a great voice of much people in heaven, saying, Alleluia; Salvation, and glory, and honour, and power, unto the Lord our God:For true and righteous are his judgments: for he hath judged the great whore, which did corrupt the earth with her fornication, and hath avenged the blood of his servants at her hand. And again they said, Alleluia. And her smoke rose up for ever and ever. And the four and twenty elders and the four beasts fell down and worshipped God that sat on the throne, saying, Amen; Alleluia. And a voice came out of the throne, saying, Praise our God, all ye his servants, and ye that fear him, both small and great. And I heard as it were the voice of a great multitude, and as the voice of many waters, and as the voice of mighty thunderings, saying, Alleluia: for the Lord God omnipotent reigneth. Let us be glad and rejoice, and give honour to him: for the marriage of the Lamb is come, and his wife hath made herself ready. And to her was granted that she should be arrayed in fine linen, clean and white: for the fine linen is the righteousness of saints." (Rev 18:24-19:8) In communion with them, the Church on earth also sings these songs with faith in the midst of trial. By means of petition and intercession, faith hopes against all hope and gives thanks to the "Father of lights," from whom "every perfect gift" comes down. Thus faith is pure praise.

The Eucharist contains and expresses all forms of prayer: it is "the pure offering" of the whole Body of Christ to the glory of God's name and, according to the traditions of East and West, it is the "sacrifice of praise." "For from the rising of the sun even unto the going down of the same my name shall be great among the Gentiles; and in every place incense shall be offered unto my name, and a pure offering: for my name shall be great among the heathen, saith the LORD of hosts." (Mal 1:11)

Prayer of Petition

The vocabulary of petition or supplication in the New Testament is rich in shades of meaning; ask, beseech, plead, invoke, entreat, cry out, even "struggle in prayer." (Rom 15:30; Col 4:12) Its most usual form, because the most spontaneous, is petition: by prayer of petition we express awareness of our relationship with God. We are creatures who are not our own beginning, not the masters of adversity, not our own last end. We are sinners who as Christians know that we have turned away from our Father. Our petition is already a turning back to him.

The New Testament contains scarcely any prayers of lamentation, so frequent in the Old Testament. In the risen Christ the Church's petition is buoyed by hope, even if we still wait in a state of expectation and must be converted anew every day. Christian petition, what St. Paul calls "groaning," arises from another depth, that of creation "in labor pains" and that of ourselves "as we wait for the redemption of our bodies. For in this hope we were saved." (Rom 8:22-24) In the end, however, "with sighs too deep for words" the Holy Spirit "helps us in our weakness; for we do not know how to pray as we ought, but the Spirit himself intercedes for us with sighs too deep for words." (Rom 8:26)

As in all prayer, the first movement of the prayer of petition is asking forgiveness, like the tax collector in the parable: "God, be merciful to me a sinner!" (Luke 18:13) It is a prerequisite for righteous and pure prayer. A trusting humility brings us back into the light of communion between the Father and his Son Jesus Christ and with one another, so that "we receive from him whatever we ask." (1Jn 3:22; cf. 1:7-2:2) Asking forgiveness is the prerequisite for both the Eucharistic liturgy and personal prayer.

Christian petition is centered on the desire and search for the Kingdom to come, in keeping with the teaching of Christ. "But seek ye first the kingdom of God, and his righteousness; and all these things shall be added unto you." (Matt 6:33) "And he said unto them, When ye pray, say, Our Father which art in heaven, Hallowed be thy name. Thy kingdom come. Thy will be done, as in heaven, so in earth. If ye then, being evil, know how to give good gifts unto your children: how much more shall your heavenly Father give the Holy Spirit to them that ask him?" (Luke 11:2, 13) There is a hierarchy in these petitions: we pray first for the Kingdom, then for what is necessary to welcome it and cooperate with it's coming. This collaboration with the mission of Christ and the Holy Spirit, which is now that of the Church, is the object of the prayer of the apostolic community. (Acts 6:6; 13:3) It is the prayer of Paul, the apostle par excellence, which reveals to us how the divine solicitude for all the churches ought to inspire Christian prayer. (Rom 10:1; Eph 1:16-23; Phil 1911; Col 1:3-6; 4:3-4, 12) By prayer every baptized person works for the coming of the Kingdom.

When we share in God's saving love, we understand that every need can become the object of petition. Christ, who assumed all things in order to redeem all things, is glorified by what we ask the Father in his name. (John 14:13) It is with this confidence that St. James and St. Paul exhort us to 'pray at all times.' "If any of you lack wisdom, let him ask of God, that giveth to all men liberally, and upbraideth not; and it shall be given him. But let him ask in faith, nothing wavering. For he that wavereth is like a wave of the sea driven with the wind and tossed. For let not that man think that he shall receive any thing of the Lord. A double minded man is unstable in all his ways." (James 1:5-8) "Giving thanks always for all things unto God and the Father in the name of our Lord Jesus Christ;" (Eph 5:20); (Phil 4:6-7; Col 3:16-17; 1 Thess 5:17-18)

Trust is tested—it proves itself—in tribulation. "And not only so, but we glory in tribulations also: knowing that tribulation worketh patience; And patience, experience; and experience, hope: And hope maketh not ashamed; because the love of God is shed abroad in our hearts by the Holy Ghost which is given unto us." (Rom 5:3-5) The principal difficulty concerns the prayer of petition, for oneself or for others in intercession. Some even stop praying because they think their petition is not heard. Here two questions should be asked: *Why do we think our petition has not been heard? How is our prayer heard, how is it "efficacious"? Further we should ask; Why do we complain of not being heard?*

In the first place, we ought to be astonished by this fact: when we praise God or give him thanks for his benefits in general, we are not particularly concerned whether or not our prayer is acceptable to him. On the other hand, we demand to see the results of our petitions. What is the image of God that motivates our prayer: an instrument to be used? or the Father of our Lord Jesus Christ? Are we convinced that "we do not know how to pray as we ought"? (Rom 8:26) Are we asking God for "what is good for us"? Our Father knows what we need before we ask him, "Be not ye therefore like unto them: for your Father knoweth what things ye have need of, before ye ask him." (Matt 6:8) But he awaits our petition because the dignity of his children lies in their freedom. We must pray, then, with his Spirit of freedom, to be able truly to know what he wants. "And he that searcheth the hearts knoweth what is the mind of the Spirit, because he maketh intercession for the saints according to the will of God." (Rom 8:27)

"You ask and do not receive, because you ask wrongly, to spend it on your passions."(James 4:3; the whole context: James 4:1-10; 1:5-8; 5:16) If we ask with a divided heart, we are "adulterers"; (James 4:4) God cannot answer us, for he desires our well-being, our life. "Or do you suppose that it is in vain that the scripture says, 'He yearns jealously over the spirit which he has made to dwell in us?'"(James 4:5) That our God is "jealous" for us is the sign of how true his love is. If we enter into the desire of his

Spirit, we shall be heard. Do not be troubled if you do not immediately receive from God what you ask him; for he desires to do something even greater for you, while you cling to him in prayer. (Evagrius Ponticus, *De oratione* 34: PG 79, 1173) God wills that our desire should be exercised in prayer, that we may be able to receive what he is prepared to give. (St. Augustine, Ep. 130, 8, 17: PL 33, 500)

The revelation of prayer in the economy of salvation teaches us that faith rests on God's action in history. Our trust is enkindled by his supreme act: the Passion and Resurrection of his Son. Christian prayer is cooperation with his providence, his plan of love for men.

For St. Paul, this trust is bold, founded on the prayer of the Spirit in us and on the faithful love of the Father who has given us his only Son. "For there is no difference between the Jew and the Greek: for the same Lord over all is rich unto all that call upon him. For whosoever shall call upon the name of the Lord shall be saved." (Rom 10:12-13)

> Likewise the Spirit also helpeth our infirmities: for we know not what we should pray for as we ought: but the Spirit itself maketh intercession for us with groanings which cannot be uttered. And he that searcheth the hearts knoweth what is the mind of the Spirit, because he maketh intercession for the saints according to the will of God. And we know that all things work together for good to them that love God, to them who are the called according to his purpose. For whom he did foreknow, he also did predestinate to be conformed to the image of his Son, that he might be the firstborn among many brethren. Moreover whom he did predestinate, them he also called: and whom he called, them he also justified: and whom he justified, them he also glorified. What shall we then say to these things? If God be for us, who can be against us? He that spared not his own Son, but delivered him up for us all, how shall he not with him also freely give us all things? Who shall lay any thing to the charge of God's elect? It is God that justifieth.

Who is he that condemneth? It is Christ that died, yea rather, that is risen again, who is even at the right hand of God, who also maketh intercession for us. Who shall separate us from the love of Christ? shall tribulation, or distress, or persecution, or famine, or nakedness, or peril, or sword? As it is written, For thy sake we are killed all the day long; we are accounted as sheep for the slaughter. Nay, in all these things we are more than conquerors through him that loved us. For I am persuaded, that neither death, nor life, nor angels, nor principalities, nor powers, nor things present, nor things to come, Nor height, nor depth, nor any other creature, shall be able to separate us from the love of God, which is in Christ Jesus our Lord." (Rom 8:26-39)

Transformation of the praying heart is the first response to our petition.

The prayer of Jesus makes Christian prayer a successful petition. He is its model, he prays in us and with us. Since the heart of the Son seeks only what pleases the Father, how could the prayer of the children of adoption be centered on the gifts rather than the Giver? Jesus also prays for us—in our place and on our behalf. All our petitions were gathered up, once for all, in his cry on the Cross and, in his Resurrection, heard by the Father. This is why he never ceases to intercede for us with the Father. "Who in the days of his flesh, when he had offered up prayers and supplications with strong crying and tears unto him that was able to save him from death, and was heard in that he feared;" (Heb 5:7) "Wherefore he is able also to save them to the uttermost that come unto God by him, seeing he ever liveth to make intercession for them." (Heb 7:25) "For Christ is not entered into the holy places made with hands, which are the figures of the true; but into heaven itself, now to appear in the presence of God for us:" (Heb 9:24) If our prayer is resolutely united with that of Jesus, in trust and boldness as children, we obtain all that we ask in his name, even more than any particular thing: the Holy Spirit himself, who contains all gifts.

Prayer of Intercession

Intercession is a unique prayer of petition that leads us to pray as Jesus did. He is the one intercessor with the Father on behalf of all men, especially sinners. "Who is he that condemneth? It is Christ that died, yea rather, that is risen again, who is even at the right hand of God, who also maketh intercession for us." (Rom 8:34) "My little children, these things write I unto you, that ye sin not. And if any man sin, we have an advocate with the Father, Jesus Christ the righteous:" (I Jn 2:1) "For there is one God, and one mediator between God and men, the man Christ Jesus; Who gave himself a ransom for all, to be testified in due time. Whereunto I am ordained a preacher, and an apostle, (I speak the truth in Christ, and lie not;) a teacher of the Gentiles in faith and verity. I will therefore that men pray every where, lifting up holy hands, without wrath and doubting." (1 Tim 2:5-8) He is "able also to save them to the uttermost that come unto God by him, seeing he ever liveth to make intercession for them." (Heb 7:25) The Holy Spirit "himself intercedes for us…and intercedes for the saints according to the will of God." (Rom 8:26-27)

Since Abraham, intercession—asking on behalf of another—has been characteristic of a heart attuned to God's mercy. In the age of the Church, Christian intercession participates in Christ's, as an expression of the communion of saints. In intercession, he who prays looks "not only to his own interests, but also to the interests of others," even to the point of praying for those who do him harm. For, we must "Look not every man on his own things, but every man also on the things of others." (Phil 2:4) "Then said Jesus, Father, forgive them; for they know not what they do. And they parted his raiment, and cast lots." (Luke 23:34)

The first Christian communities lived this form of fellowship intensely. For we know that "Peter therefore was kept in prison: but prayer was made without ceasing of the church unto God for him." (Acts 12:5) "And when we had accomplished those days, we departed and went our way; and they all brought us on our way, with wives and children, till we were out of the city: and we kneeled down on the shore, and prayed." (Acts 21:5) "And by their prayer for you, which long after you for the exceeding grace of God in you." (2Cor 9:14)

Thus the Apostle Paul gives them a share in his ministry of preaching the Gospel "Praying always with all prayer and supplication in the Spirit, and watching thereunto with all perseverance and supplication for all saints;" (Eph 6:18) But he also intercedes for them. "Wherefore also we pray always for you, that our God would count you worthy of this calling, and fulfill all the good pleasure of his goodness, and the work of faith with power:" (2Thess 1:11) "We give thanks to God and the Father of our Lord Jesus Christ, praying always for you," (Col 1:3) The intercession of Christians recognizes no boundaries: "for all men, for kings and all who are in high positions," for persecutors, for the salvation of those who reject the Gospel. (Rom 12:14)

Intercessory prayers continued in very early liturgical pronouncements: *The Divine Liturgy of Saint James*, The Holy Apostle and Brother of the Lord, the liturgy of the church of Jerusalem, AD150-200; *The Divine Liturgy of the Holy Apostle and Evangelist Mark*, the Disciple of the Holy Peter, the liturgy of the church of Alexandria, AD150-200; *The Liturgy of the Blessed Apostles*, Composed by St. Adaeus and St. Maris, Teachers of the Easterns, one of the three Nestorian Liturgies, AD150, and others. For example, we find these words in the *Epistle of Ignatius to the Ephesians*, Chapter IX AD 107, "And pray ye without ceasing in behalf of other men. For there is in them hope of repentance, that they may attain to God."

In a later document, *The Testament of Abraham*; (the Paris Manuscript written in Greek, in 1315 with reference to Greek texts written in the second century receiving its present form in the ninth century) assumed to be written by a Jewish Christian in the Egyptian style of the period, we find that intercession on behalf of others can have the ultimate influence with our Lord. "And Abraham said to the chief-captain, My lord the chief-captain, the shield which the angel held in his hand, why was it adjudged to be set in the midst? The chief-captain said, Listen, righteous Abraham. Because the judge found its sins and its righteousness equal, he neither committed it to judgment nor to be saved, until the judge of all shall come. Abraham said to the chief-captain, And what yet is wanting for the soul to be saved? The chief-captain said, If it obtains one righteousness above its sins, it enters into salvation. Abraham said to the chief-captain, Come hither, chief-captain Michael, let us make prayer for this soul, and see whether God will hear us. The chief-captain said, Amen, be it so; and they made prayer and entreaty for the soul, and God heard them, and when they rose up from their prayer they did not see the soul standing there. And Abraham said to the angel, Where is the soul that thou didst hold in the midst? And the angel answered, It has been saved by thy righteous prayer, and behold an angel of light has taken it and carried it up into Paradise."

For many people such intercessory prayer is particularly difficult. If God knows what is going to happen anyway, what is the point of asking? The important point to grasp is the fact of co-operation. In ordinary daily life God works through our cooperation. Clearly God is allowing us to influence the course of events, but what of intercessory prayer? Such prayer is not a technique for changing God's mind, but is a releasing of God's power through the placing of us in a relationship of co-operation with God. It is a direct and positive act—it takes effort, persistence, caring for others AND a particularly strong "Faith". Prayer and action should not be opposed to each other, for prayer is action. **Intercession means literally to stand between, to become involved in the conflict.**

In the Old Testament the prayer of intercession is a redemptive work, a priestly act of identifying oneself with the sufferings of the people. So Abraham intercedes for Sodom

> "And the men rose up from thence, and looked toward Sodom: and Abraham went with them to bring them on the way. And the LORD said, Shall I hide from Abraham that thing which I do; Seeing that Abraham shall surely become a great and mighty nation, and all the nations of the earth shall be blessed in him? For I know him, that he will command his children and his household after him, and they shall keep the way of the LORD, to do justice and judgment; that the LORD may bring upon Abraham that which he hath spoken of him. And the LORD said, Because the cry of Sodom and Gomorrah is great, and because their sin is very grievous; I will go down now, and see whether they have done altogether according to the cry of it, which is come unto me; and if not, I will know.
>
> And the men turned their faces from thence, and went toward Sodom: but Abraham stood yet before the LORD. And Abraham drew near, and said, Wilt thou also destroy the righteous with the wicked? Peradventure there be fifty righteous within the city: wilt thou also destroy and not spare the place for the fifty righteous that are therein? That be far from thee to do after this manner, to slay the righteous with the wicked: and that the righteous should be as the wicked, that be far from thee: Shall not the Judge of all the earth do right? And the LORD said, If I find in Sodom fifty righteous within the city, then I will spare all the place for their sakes. And Abraham answered and said, Behold now, I have taken upon me to speak unto the Lord, which am but dust and ashes: Peradventure there shall lack five of the fifty righteous: wilt thou destroy all

the city for lack of five? And he said, If I find there forty and five, I will not destroy it. And he spake unto him yet again, and said, Peradventure there shall be forty found there. And he said, I will not do it for forty's sake. And he said unto him, Oh let not the Lord be angry, and I will speak: Peradventure there shall thirty be found there. And he said, I will not do it, if I find thirty there. And he said, Behold now, I have taken upon me to speak unto the Lord: Peradventure there shall be twenty found there. And he said, I will not destroy it for twenty's sake. And he said, Oh let not the Lord be angry, and I will speak yet but this once: Peradventure ten shall be found there. And he said, I will not destroy it for ten's sake." (Gen 18:16-32)

Moses lifts up his hands to intercede for Israel
"And it came to pass, when Moses held up his hand, that Israel prevailed: and when he let down his hand, Amalek prevailed. But Moses' hands were heavy; and they took a stone, and put it under him, and he sat thereon; and Aaron and Hur stayed up his hands, the one on the one side, and the other on the other side; and his hands were steady until the going down of the sun." (Exod 17:11-12)

...and prays that God would be with his people
"And he said, If now I have found grace in thy sight, O Lord, let my Lord, I pray thee, go among us; for it is a stiffnecked people; and pardon our iniquity and our sin, and take us for thine inheritance." (Exod 34:9)

In Ezekiel, the oppression and falsehood cause God to state that he looked for someone to stand in the breach to stop the destruction....but did not find anyone to be the intercessor, "And I sought for a man among them, that should make up the hedge, and stand in the gap before me for the land, that I should not destroy it: but I found none." (Ezek 22:30)

In Second Isaiah He found no intercessor, "And he saw that there was no man, and wondered that there was no intercessor:" (Isa 59:16)

Again, the work of intercession is closely linked with the theme of redemptive suffering "Therefore will I divide him a portion with the great, and he shall divide the spoil with the strong; because he hath poured out his soul unto death: and he was numbered with the transgressors; and he bare the sin of many, and made intercession for the transgressors." (Isa 53:12)

Intercession certainly is not just for the intentions of the sick. Intercession is simply our co-operation with God in the work of reconciliation. It is like all prayer, God centered, but in intercession this fact needs to be stressed more strongly, in view of the danger of focusing on the people for whom we pray. We must see their needs in the context of a wider vision rather than selfish individualism.

Since it is the duty of all saints to pray for one another, we intercede and ask the supplications of our friends, the Saints in heaven, and our parish family. The Prayers of the People at the Eucharistic Liturgy are excellent guides for interceding on another's behalf.

I can't imagine a Christian going through life without praying for someone else. With this form of prayer we pray as Jesus did. "He is the one intercessor with the Father on behalf of all men, especially sinners." (Rom. 8:34; 1Jn 2:1; 1Tim 2:5-8) Now someone may ask, "Why pray for a sinner when Jesus is the one intercessor?" or, as some would phrase it, "How can the saints intercede for us when Jesus is the one mediator?" The answer to both these questions can be found in the Greek term used for "one." It is my understanding that the term used by St. Paul does not mean "one and only" (mono in Greek) but "primary one." (heis in Greek) Therefore, we can intercede in Jesus as members of His Body, along with the saints. Thus Christian intercession participates in Christ's, as an expression of the Communion of Saints.

An intercessor is a man or woman—or child—who fights on behalf of others, as such; intercession is the activity that identifies us most with Christ.

Intercession as opposed to simple prayers

1. Asks God for divine intervention

2. Destroys the works of Satan.

Developing a watchman's eye…..general preparation

1. Tell the Lord that you are willing to be a watchman

2. Keep your heart pure so that you can properly discern areas for which God wants you to pray.

3. Be aware at every moment that you are on call

4. God reveals to intercessors the intimate needs of those for whom we intercede. This is a precious trust. If God reveals the needs of another to you, you must
   - Ask for confirmation,
   - Ask if you should tell the person what you have learned,
   - Ask that God prepare the heart of the receiver,
   - If the issues are so great, go to your minister and leave it in his hands

5. Do not be afraid to pray prayers that may seem unusual to you…ie, that you pray for those that you do not know.

Luke 22:31-32
"Simon, Simon, Satan has asked to sift you as wheat.
But I have prayed for you, Simon, that your faith may not fail. And when you have turned back, strengthen your brothers."

Prayer of Meditation

Possibly the clearest example of the vital place of prayer was the life and ministry of the hermit. St. Anthony, the first and most renowned Desert Father practicing a life of meditation and contemplation and living in the Egyptian desert was greatly loved and admired by the Celtic Church. The ancient high crosses of Monasterboice in Ireland are carved with two saints—Anthony and Paul of Thebes, both Desert Fathers. (Cuthbert, Eadbert, Aidan, etc.)

Quiet meditative prayer enables us to fulfill two commands given in the Psalms: (1) "Be still and know;" (Psalm 46:10) and (2) "Taste and see." (Psalm 34:8). In other words, minds that are blind and deaf and mute to all things except the holy name of Jesus.

> As we read in *Cassian's Conferences, The First Conference of Abbot Isaac on Prayer,* Chapter XXXV, AD495:
> "Before all things however we ought most carefully to observe the Evangelic precept, which tells us to enter into our chamber and shut the door and pray to our Father, which may be fulfilled by us as follows: We pray within our chamber, when removing our hearts inwardly from the din of all thoughts and anxieties, we disclose our prayers in secret and in closest intercourse to the Lord. We pray with closed doors when with closed lips and complete silence we pray to the searcher not of words but of hearts. We pray in secret when from the heart and

fervent mind we disclose our petitions to God alone, so that no hostile powers are even able to discover the character of our petition. Wherefore we should pray in complete silence, not only to avoid distracting the brethren standing near by our whispers or louder utterances, and disturbing the thoughts of those who are praying but also that the purport of our petition may be concealed from our enemies who are especially on the watch against us while we are praying. For who we shall fulfill this injunction: 'Keep the doors of the mouth from her who sleepeth in thy bosom.'"

Meditation is above all a quest. The mind seeks to understand the why and how of the Christian life, in order to adhere and respond to what the Lord is asking. The required attentiveness is difficult to sustain. We are usually helped by books, and Christians do not want for them: the Sacred Scriptures, particularly the Gospels, holy icons, liturgical texts of the day or season, writings of the spiritual fathers, works of spirituality, the great book of creation, and that of history the page on which the "today" of God is written.

We are to emulate the faithful, *Meditatio Scripturarum*; "But his delight is in the law of the LORD; and in his law doth he meditate day and night." (Ps 1:2) This is different than studying Scripture centering on exegesis, but rather *internalizing and personalizing the love contained in the passages*. We must do all things to reduce our ego, our belief in rational behavior. To be quiet, to kneel in supplication, to bow one's head, to slowly read Scripture; all passages, regardless of our preferences, and to read the same passage again and again…yes, beyond your mind saying "enough already" and moving to your "comprehending heart." This type of prayer requires the mind descending into the heart…to be overcome by the imagination totally dependent upon our Lord… *lectio divina* (divine reading)..we seek the "Word exposed in the Words" (Karl Barth).

To meditate on what we read helps us to make it our own by confronting it with ourselves. Here, another book is opened: the book of life. We pass from thoughts to reality. To the extent that we are humble and faithful, we discover in meditation the movements that stir the heart and we are able to discern them. It is a question of acting truthfully in order to come into the light: "Lord, what do you want me to do?"

There are as many and varied methods of meditation as there are spiritual masters. Christians owe it to themselves to develop the desire to meditate regularly, lest they come to resemble the three first kinds of soil in the parable of the sower. (Mt 4:4-7, 15-19) But a method is only a guide; the important thing is to advance, with the Holy Spirit, along the one way of prayer: Christ Jesus.

Meditation engages thought, imagination, emotion, and desire. This mobilization of faculties is necessary in order to deepen our convictions of faith, prompt the conversion of our heart, and strengthen our will to follow Christ. Christian prayer tries above all to meditate on the mysteries of Christ, as in *lectio divina* or the rosary. This form of prayerful reflection is of great value, but Christian prayer should go further: to the knowledge of the love of the Lord Jesus, to union with him.

One thinks of the methods of St. Ignatius, St. Teresa of Avila and St. Jean Baptist de la Salle. Just to touch on one of these let's look at the Ignatian method. First, begin with the remote preparation (usually done the night before) of the subject of the meditation with some specific points that you will be considering. During the actual time of meditation begin by recalling to mind the subject you want to consider, use the imagination to picture the scene and ask God for a special grace from this meditation. In the body of the meditation ask yourself questions about the subject you are considering and perhaps come up with some answers. During the course of the meditation make acts of love (affective acts), especially at the end. After each point of the meditation you are considering make some practical resolution. End the meditation with short and intimate conversations with Jesus, Mary or the saints.

Carefully review the entire meditation and conclude with a practical resolution for your life drawn from the subject considered.

There is also a very simple and helpful method known as C.A.R. It's something like this:

- Consider—perhaps a Gospel passage.
- Apply—the passage to your life.
- Resolve—make a resolution based on the application of a the passage to your life.

Methods of meditation can be a great help but are simply a guide. We must also let the Holy Spirit guide us as He wills. Meditation engages thought, imagination, emotion and desire. This mobilization of faith prompts the conversion of our heart and strengthens our will to follow Christ. We will address specific methods later in this text.

Meditation is not only thinking or pondering. It is a consideration that leads us somewhere—or rather to someone. "This form of prayerful reflection is of great value, but Christian prayer should go further: to the knowledge of the love of the Lord Jesus, to union with Him."

In some degree or other it has always been practiced by God-fearing souls. There is abundant evidence of this in the Old Testament, as, for instance, in Ps. 38:4; 62:7; 76:13; 118 throughout; Ecclus.14:22; Is.26:9;57:1; Jer.12:11. In the New Testament Christ gave frequent examples of it, and St. Paul often refers to it, as in Eph.6:18; Col.4:2; 1Tim.4:15; 1Cor.14:15. It has always been practiced in the Church. Among others who have recommended it to the faithful as Chrysostom in his two books on prayer, as also in his "Homily xxx in Gen." and "Homily vi. in Isaiam"; Cassian in "Conference ix"; St. Jerome in "Epistola xxii ad Eustochium"; St. Basil in his "Homily on St. Julitta, M.", and "In regular breviori", 301; St. Cyprian, "In expositione orationis dominicalis"; St.

Ambrose, "De sacramentis", VI, iii; St. Augustine, "Epist. 121 ad Probam", cc. v, vi, vii; Boctius, "De spiritu et anima", xxxii; St. Leo, "Sermo viii de jejunio"; St. Bernard, "De consecratione'", I, vii; St. Thomas, II-II, Q. lxxxiii, a. 2.

The writings of the Fathers themselves and of the great theologians are in large measure the fruit of devout meditation as well as of study of the mysteries of religion. *There is, however, no trace of methodical meditation before the fifteenth century.* Prior to that time, even in monasteries, no regulation seems to have existed for the choir or arrangement of subject, the order, method, and time of the consideration. From the beginning, before the middle of the twelfth century, the Carthusians had times set apart for mental prayer, as appears from Guigo's "Consuetudinary", but no further regulation. About the beginning of the sixteenth century Brussels issued a series of subjects or points for meditation. The monastic rules generally prescribed times for common prayer, usually the recitation of the Office, leaving it to the individual to ponder as he might on one or other of the texts. Early in the sixteenth century the Dominican chapter of Milan prescribed mental prayer for half an hour morning and evening. Among the Franciscans there is record of methodical mental prayer about the middle of that century. Among the Carmelites there was no regulation for it until Saint Theresa introduced it for two hours daily. Although Saint Ignatius reduced meditation to such a definite method in his spiritual exercises, it was not made part of his rule until thirty years after the formation of the Society. His method and that of St. Sulpice have helped to spread the habit of meditating beyond the cloister among the faithful everywhere

In the method of St. Ignatius the subject of the meditation is chosen beforehand, usually the previous evening. It may be any truth or fact whatever concerning God or the human soul, God's existence His attributes, such as justice, mercy, love, wisdom, His law, providence, revelation, creation and its purpose, sin and its penalties, death, creation and its purpose, sin and its penalties, death, judgment, hell, redemption, etc. The precise aspect of the subject should be determined very definitely, otherwise its consideration will be general or superficial and of no practical benefit. As far as possible its application to one's spiritual needs should be foreseen, and to work up interest in it, as one retires and rises, one should recall it to mind so as to make it a sleeping and a waking thought.

When ready for meditation, a few moments should be given to recollecting what we are about to do so as to begin with quiet of mind and deeply impressed with the sacredness of prayer.

A brief act of adoration of God naturally follows, with a petition that our intention to honor Him in prayer may be sincere and persevering, and that every faculty and act, interior and exterior, may contribute to His service and praise. The subject of the meditation is then recalled to mind, and in order to fix the attention, the imagination is here employed to construct some scene appropriate to the subject, e.g. the Garden of Paradise, if the meditation is on Creation, or the Fall of Man; the Valley of Jehosaphat, for the Last Judgment; or, for Hell, the bottomless and boundless pit of fire. This is called *the composition of the place*, and even when the subject of meditation has no apparent material associations, the imagination can always devise some scene or sensible image that will help to fix or recall one's attention and appreciate the spiritual matter under consideration. Thus, when considering sin, especially carnal sin, as enslaving the soul, the Book of Wisdom, ix, 15, suggests the similarity of the body to the prison house of the soul: "The corruptible body is a load upon the soul, and the earthly habitation presseth down the mind that museth upon many things."

Quite often this initial step, or prelude as it is called, might occupy one profitably the entire time set apart for meditation; but ordinarily it should be made in a few minutes.

A brief petition follows for the special grace one hopes to obtain and then the meditation proper begins. The memory recalls the subject as definitely as possible, one point at a time, repeating it over if necessary, always as a matter of intimate personal interest, and with a strong act of faith until the intellect naturally apprehends the truth or the import of the fact under consideration, and begins to conceive it as a matter for careful consideration, reasoning about it and studying what it implies for one's welfare.

Gradually an intense interest is aroused in these reflections, until, with faith quickening the mind one begins to perceive applications of the truth or fact to one's condition and needs and to feel the advantage or necessity of acting upon the conclusions drawn from one's reflections. This is the important moment of meditation. The conviction that we need or should do something in accordance with our consideration creates in us desires or resolutions that we long to accomplish. It we are serious we admit no self-deception either as to the correctness or possibility of such resolutions on our part. No matter what it may cost us to be consistent, we should adopt them, and the more we appreciate their difficulty and our own weakness or incapacity, the more we should try to value the motives which prompt us to adopt them, and above all the more we should pray for grace to be able to carry them out.

If we are in earnest we should not be satisfied with a superficial process. In the light of the truth we are meditating, our past experience will come to mind and confront us perhaps with memory of failure in previous attempts similar to those we are considering now, or at least with a keen sense of the difficulty to be apprehended, making us more attentive to the our probable motives and humble in petitioning God's grace. These petitions, as well as all the various emotions that arise from our reflections, find expression in terms of prayer to God that are called colloquies, or conversations with Him. They may occur at any point in the process, whenever our thoughts inspire us to call upon God for our needs, or even for light to perceive and appreciate them and to know the means of obtaining them.

This general process is subject to variations according to the character of the matter under consideration. The number of preludes and colloquies may vary, and the time spent in reasoning may be greater or less according to our familiarity with the subject. There is nothing mechanical in the process; indeed, if analyzed, it is clearly the natural operation of each faculty and of all in concert. Roothaan, who has prepared the best summary of it, recommends a remote preparation for it, so as to know whether we are properly disposed to enter into meditation, and, after each exercise, a brief review of each part of it in detail to see how far we may have succeeded. It is strongly advised to select as a means of recalling the leading thought or motive or affection some brief memorandum, preferably couched in the words of some text of Scripture, the "Imitation of Christ", the Fathers of the Church, or of some accredited writer on spiritual things. Meditation made regularly according to this method tends to create an atmosphere or spirit of prayer.

The method in vogue among the Sulpicians and followed by the students in their seminaries is not substantially different from this. According to Chenart, companion of Olier and for a long time director of the Seminary of St. Sulpice, the meditation should consist of three parts: *(1) the preparation, (2) the prayer proper, and (3) the conclusion.*

(1) Preparation. By way of preparation we should begin with acts of adoration of Almighty God, of self-humiliation, and with fervent petition to be directed by the Holy Spirit in our prayer to know how to make it well and obtain its fruits.

(2) The Prayer Proper. The prayer proper consists of considerations and the spiritual emotions or affections that result from such considerations. Whatever the subject of the meditation may be, it should be considered as it may have been exemplified in the life of Christ, in itself, and in its practical importance for us. The simpler these considerations are the better. A long or intricate course of reasoning is not at all desirable. When some reasoning is needed, it should be simple and always in the light of faith. Speculation, subtlety, curiosity are all out of place.

(3) Conclusion. Plain, practical reflections, always with an eye to self-examination, in order to see how well or poorly our conduct conforms to the conclusions we derive from such reflections, are the targets sought.

Prayer of Contemplation

Silent contemplative prayer (Hesychia) is the process of the mature prayer because of its complexity and its demands of the prayer.

No less than three times in the Bible we find the words: "And it shall come to pass, that whosoever shall call on the name of the Lord (prayer) shall be saved." (Acts 2:21, Romans 10:13, Joel 2:23). "Whoever walks the road, although a fool, shall not go astray." The assurance has been given us, then, that no harm can come to us in the practice of quiet contemplative prayer. But that is only a secondary meaning to these words. The pointed use of the term *"fool"* which means one who is simple-minded, without intellectuality or cleverness at all—does not indicate stupidity but rather indicates *the utter simplicity of the practice of contemplative prayer.* "Let no man deceive himself. If any man among you seemeth to be wise in this world, let him become a fool, that he may be wise" (1Cor 3:18).

"And the ransomed of the Lord shall return, and come to Zion with songs and everlasting joy upon their heads." This method of interior prayer is the process of return—the reawakening to the knowledge of our true nature as prodigal sons of God, and the return to the bosom of the Father (Luke 15:18) This is true repentance, for the word *metanoia*, so translated, actually means reversal, a complete turning around, and not a mere emotion or regret for past actions.

Contemplative prayer produces a true, saving condition of repentance-return. Even more, this way of prayer is the true religion, for that term is a translation of the Latin word religere, which means "to bind back: It is deep, contemplative prayer which reunites the strayed consciousness of the individual to its infinite Source, restoring the lost unity.

First, it restores man to his primal condition of being omologos, which literally means "one worded" or "one thoughted" in Greek. It produces the desirable state of being single-minded in contrast to our present condition of "double-mindedness" censured by Saint James, "A double minded man is unstable in all his ways…purify your hearts, ye double minded (Js. 1:8, 4:8b).

Second, contemplative prayer is an ascent to the Divine because it involves the continual invocation of the Divine Name. It is not the Name itself that has an inherent power, but rather He Who is invoked—as well as the Christian who is empowered to wield that Name as a divine sword to cut off all fleshly ties and earthly distractions from the mind. Further, it is the Holy Spirit who is praying through us in this prayer, for "No man can say 'Lord Jesus' except by the Holy Spirit" (1Cor 12:3). Only he who understands contemplative prayer understands the full meaning of the Lord Jesus' words: "I am the way, the truth, and the life: no man cometh unto the Father, but by me." (John 14:6).

So what, exactly, is contemplative prayer? St. Teresa answers: "Contemplative prayer [*oracion mental*] in my opinion is nothing else than a close sharing between friends; it means taking time frequently to be alone with him who we know loves us." (St. Teresa of Jesus, The Book of Her Life, 8, 5 in *The Collected Works of St. Teresa of Avila*, tr. K. Kavanaugh, OCD, and O. Rodriguez, OCD, Washington DC: Institute of Carmelite Studies, 1976) Contemplative prayer seeks him "whom my soul loves." (Song 1:7) It is Jesus, and in him, the Father. We seek him, because to desire him is always the beginning of love, and we seek him in that pure faith which causes us to be born of him and to live in him. In this inner prayer we can still meditate, but our attention is fixed on the Lord himself.

The choice of the time and duration of the prayer arises from a determined will, revealing the secrets of the heart. One does not undertake contemplative prayer only when one has the time: one makes time for the Lord, with the firm determination not to give up, no matter what trials and dryness one may encounter. One cannot always meditate, but one can always enter into inner prayer, independently of the conditions of health, work, or emotional state. The heart is the place of this quest and encounter, in poverty and in faith.

Entering into contemplative prayer is like entering into the Eucharistic liturgy: we "gather up:" the heart, recollect our whole being under the prompting of the Holy Spirit, abide in the dwelling place of the Lord which we are, awaken our faith in order to enter into the presence of him who awaits us. We let our masks fall and turn our hearts back to the Lord who loves us, so as to hand ourselves over to him as an offering to be purified and transformed.

Contemplative prayer is the prayer of the child of God, of the forgiven sinner who agrees to welcome the love by which he is loved and who wants to respond to it by loving even more.

> "But wisdom is justified of all her children. And one of the Pharisees desired him that he would eat with him. And he went into the Pharisee's house, and sat down to meat. And, behold, a woman in the city, which was a sinner, when she knew that Jesus sat at meat in the Pharisee's house, brought an alabaster box of ointment, And stood at his feet behind him weeping, and began to wash his feet with tears, and did wipe them with the hairs of her head, and kissed his feet, and anointed them with the ointment.
>
> Now when the Pharisee which had bidden him saw it, he spake within himself, saying, This man, if he were a prophet, would have known who and what manner of woman this is that toucheth him: for she is a sinner. And Jesus answering said unto him, Simon, I have somewhat to say unto thee. And he saith, Master, say on.

There was a certain creditor which had two debtors: the one owed five hundred pence, and the other fifty. And when they had nothing to pay, he frankly forgave them both. Tell me therefore, which of them will love him most? Simon answered and said, I suppose that he, to whom he forgave most. And he said unto him, Thou hast rightly judged. And he turned to the woman, and said unto Simon, Seest thou this woman? I entered into thine house, thou gavest me no water for my feet: but she hath washed my feet with tears, and wiped them with the hairs of her head. Thou gavest me no kiss: but this woman since the time I came in hath not ceased to kiss my feet. My head with oil thou didst not anoint: but this woman hath anointed my feet with ointment. Wherefore I say unto thee, Her sins, which are many, are forgiven; for she loved much: but to whom little is forgiven, the same loveth little. And he said unto her, Thy sins are forgiven.

And they that sat at meat with him began to say within themselves, Who is this that forgiveth sins also? And he said to the woman, Thy faith hath saved thee; go in peace." (Luke 7:35-50)

"And Jesus entered and passed through Jericho. And, behold, there was a man named Zacchaeus, which was the chief among the publicans, and he was rich. And he sought to see Jesus who he was; and could not for the press, because he was little of stature. And he ran before, and climbed up into a sycomore tree to see him: for he was to pass that way.

And when Jesus came to the place, he looked up, and saw him, and said unto him, Zacchaeus, make haste, and come down; for to day I must abide at thy house. And he made haste, and came down, and received him joyfully. And when they saw it, they all murmured, saying, That he was gone to be guest with a man that is a sinner.

And Zacchaeus stood, and said unto the Lord; Behold, Lord, the half of my goods I give to the poor; and if I have taken any thing from any man by false accusation, I restore him fourfold. And Jesus said unto him, This day is salvation come to this house, forsomuch as he also is a son of Abraham. For the Son of man is come to seek and to save that which was lost." (Luke 19:1-10)

But he knows that the Spirit in his heart pours out the love he is returning, for everything is grace from God. Contemplative prayer is the poor and humble surrender to the loving will of the Father in ever-deeper union with his beloved Son.

Once learned, contemplative prayer can be the simplest expression of the mystery of prayer. It is a gift, a grace; it can be accepted only in humility and poverty. Contemplative prayer is a covenant relationship established by God within our hearts. "But this shall be the covenant that I will make with the house of Israel; After those days, saith the LORD, I will put my law in their inward parts, and write it in their hearts; and will be their God, and they shall be my people." (Jer 31:33) Contemplative prayer is a communion in which the Holy Trinity conforms man, the image of God, "to his likeness."

Contemplative prayer is also the pre-eminently intense time of prayer. In it the Father strengthens our inner being with power through his Spirit "that Christ may dwell in [our] hearts through faith" and we may be "grounded in love." (Eph 3:16-17)

Contemplation is a gaze of faith, fixed on Jesus. "I look at him and he looks at me": this is what a certain peasant of Ars used to say to his holy cure about his prayer before the tabernacle. This focus on Jesus is a renunciation of self. His gaze purifies our heart; the light of the countenance of Jesus illumines the eyes of our heart and teaches us to see everything in the light of his truth and his compassion for all men. Contemplation also turns its gaze on the mysteries of the life of Christ.

Thus it learns the "interior knowledge of our Lord," the more to love him and follow him. (St. Ignatius Loyola, *Spiritual Exercises*, p104)

It is hearing the Word of God. Far from being passive, such attentiveness is the obedience of faith, the unconditional acceptance of a servant, and the loving commitment of a child. It participates in the "Yes" of the Son become servant and the Fiat of God's lowly handmaid.

It is silence, the "symbol of the world to come" (St. Isaac of Nineveh, *Tract. myst.* 66) or "silent love." (St. John of the Cross, Maxims and Counsels, 53 in *The Collected Works of St. John of the Cross*, tr. K. Kavanaugh, OCD, and O. Rodriguez, OCD (Washington DC: Institute of Carmelite Studies, 1979). Words in this kind of prayer are not speeches; they are like kindling that feeds the fire of love. In this silence, unbearable to the "outer" man, the Father speaks to us his incarnate Word, who suffered, died, and rose; in this silence the Spirit of adoption enables us to share in the prayer of Jesus.

Contemplative prayer is a union with the prayer of Christ insofar as it makes us participate in his mystery. The Church in the Eucharist celebrates the mystery of Christ, and the Holy Spirit makes it come alive in contemplative prayer so that our charity will manifest it in our acts.

It is a communion of love bearing Life for the multitude, to the extent that it consents to abide in the night of faith. The Paschal night of the Resurrection passes through the night of the agony and the tomb—the three intense moments of the Hour of Jesus that his Spirit (and not "the flesh [which] is weak") brings to life in prayer. We must be willing to "keep watch with [him] one hour." (Mt 26:40)

Contemplative prayer immerses us into the silence of god

But this type of prayer is for the mature pray-er. Some of the indicators are suggested to be:
- Continuing hunger for intimacy with God
- An ability to forgive others at great personal cost, a living sense that God alone can satisfy the longings of the human heart

- A deep satisfaction in prayer
- A realistic assessment of personal abilities and shortcomings
- A freedom from boasting about spiritual accomplishments
- A demonstrated ability to live out the demands of life patiently and wisely

This type of prayer may be described as of God's Spirit and not of man's invention.

Steps that might be used in this prayer are listed below. If your retreat master, the priest-in-charge of your retreat or your parish priest (if you are contemplating this little book in private) believes that you are sufficiently mature to attempt this prayer style then take a moment an jot down your reflections to each of the following statements. You should be able to respond completely and with quiet confidence to each suggestion!

- You may begin with a simple breadth prayer...Abba, Father...or another
- You can control distractions by always returning to the rhythm of the breadth prayer
- You can diminish your worry over your inability to "warm" to our Lord by simply inviting the Lord into your heart.
- The best option is to pray in a Celtic manner...in the reality of life the prayer of St. Aidan provides an example.
  God is within
  God in my head and my thinking
  God in my eyes and in my seeing
  God in my mouth and in my speaking
  God in my heart and my loving
  God in my hands and in each action
  God in my feet and on each journey
  God within me and without me

> *God in the heart of friend and stranger*
> *God in the other who comes to me (David Adam, Flame in My Heart)*

- Also to pray in the Celtic manner to call upon the Trinity

> *The compassing of God and His right hand*
> *Be upon my form and upon my frame;*
> *The compassing of the High King and the grace of the Trinity*
> *Be upon me abiding ever eternally,*
> *Be upon me abiding ever eternally. (Esther de Waal, The Celtic Vision)*

If you use an alternative, repetitive style of prayer jot it down below. You will be able to compare this approach to others as time passes and your prayer life continues to mature

Unceasing Prayer

Although born a British Celt, St. Patrick, evangelist, pastor and bishop, was captured by Irish slave traders and sold to a chieftain named Milch. He was put to work herding cattle in County Antrim and here he found our Lord Jesus Christ. It was on the slopes of Slemish near Ballymeana, that Patrick experienced an extraordinary surge of prayer, as he records in his "Confession,"

> But after I had come to Ireland I daily used to feed cattle, and I prayed frequently during the day/ the love of God and the fear of Him increased more and more, and faith became strong, and the spirit was stirred that in one day I said about a hundred prayers, and in the night nearly the same; so that I used even to remain in the woods and in the mountains; before daylight I used to rise to prayer, through snow, through frost, through rain, and I felt no harm; nor was there any slothfulness in me, as I now perceive, because the sprit was then fervent within me.
> (The Confession of Patrick, quoted in Noel O'Donoghue, *Aristocracy of the Soul,* 1987, 105).

The prayer life of the early Celtic Church is worthy of the admiration of Christians of every tradition. In our church heritage you find contemplative hermits leading austere lives of fasting and contemplative prayer.

You also find Pentecostal enthusiastic prayer. Perhaps the Celtic Church, more than any other, was true to St. Paul's exhortation to the Ephesisans, to "pray in the Spirit on all occasions with all kinds of prayers and requests." (Eph 6:18)

We read in the *Homily Concerning Lowliness of Mind; and Commentary on Philippians*, St. Chrysostom AD387, "For things which often we have not strength to perform successfully from our won exertions, these we shall have power to accomplish easily through prayers. I mean prayers which are persevering. For always and without intermission it is a duty to pray. Hast thou not been heart? Persevere, in order that thou mayest be heard."

"And, therefore, while it is still glowing the prayer is to be snatched as speedily as possible out of the jaws of the enemy, who, although he is indeed always hostile to us, is yet never more hostile than when he sees that we are anxious to offer up prayers to God against his attacks; and by exciting wandering thoughts and all sorts of rumors he (Satan) endeavors to distract our minds from attending to our prayers, and by this means tries to make it grow cold, though begun with fervor. Wherefore they think it best for the prayers to be short and offered up very frequently: on the one hand that by so often praying to the Lord we may be able to cleave to Him continually; on the other, that when the devil is lying in wait for us, we may by their terse brevity avoid the darts with which he endeavors to wound us especially when we are saying our prayers." *The Twelve Books of John Cassian on the Institutes of the Coenobia;* Book II, **Of the Canonical System of the Nocturnal Prayers and Psalms,** Chapter X, AD495

> We read further in *The Epistles of Cyprian, Epistle VII, To the Clergy, Concerning Prayer to God,* AD258.
>
> "Let us urgently pray and groan with continual petitions......Let us therefore strike off and break away from the bonds of sleep, and pray with urgency and watchfulness, as the Apostle Paul bids us.....

'Continue in prayer, and watch in the same with thanksgiving; Withal praying also for us, that God would open unto us a door of utterance, to speak the mystery of Christ,'
(Col 4:2-3)

For the apostles also ceased not to pray day and night and the Lord also Himself, the teacher of our discipline, and the way of our example, frequently and watchfully prayed, as we read in the Gospel…

'And it came to pass in those days, that he went out into a mountain to pray, and continued all night in prayer to God.'
(Luke 6:12)

But He so prayed for us

'And the Lord said, Simon, Simon, behold, Satan hath desired to have you, that he may sift you as wheat: But I have prayed for thee, that thy faith fail not: and when thou art converted, strengthen thy brethren.'
(Luke 22:31-32)

But if for us and for our sins He both labored and watched and prayed, how much more ought we to be instant in prayers; and, first of all, to pray and to entreat the Lord Himself, and then through Him, to make satisfaction to God the Father!"

The parable of the "importunate widow" is one of the three principal parables on prayer, (Luke 18:1-8) This parable begins with the exhortation from Jesus to "always pray and not lose heart." Jesus tells us about a judge who fears neither God nor respects man. A widow keeps coming to this judge pleading for justice against an adversary for a long time. Finally, the judge accedes to her because otherwise she will wear him out. Jesus concludes by saying that God will avenge quickly His elect who cry to Him day and night. He adds, "When the Son of Man comes, will he find, do you think, faith on the earth?" The parable is centered on one of the qualities of prayer. "It is necessary to pray always without ceasing and with the patience of faith." This exhortation to pray always is echoed in the words of St. Paul to the Thessalonians. (1Th. 5,17)

So we are told in Sacred Scripture to pray without ceasing. But in Saint Matthew we are advised not to rattle on like the pagans by multiplying words. (Mt. 6:7-8) What are we to make of this? St. Augustine, one of the great Fathers of the Church, offers us two solutions. He tells us that one way of praying always is to cherish a holy desire. "We must always yearn for God in our hearts." (*Sermon* 9,3) If our desire for God is uninterrupted so is our prayer according to him. If praying means kneeling, prostrating or lifting up our hands to heaven then St. Augustine does not think we can always do it. But interior prayer, the desire of the heart, this we can do ceaselessly according to him.

The second way St. Augustine suggests for 'praying always' is by continuous right living. He realistically points out that nobody's tongue could endure praising God all day long. (Although I know some people who talk so much they could prove him wrong!) But in all that we do, if we do it well, we have praised God. (Ps. 34-2nd-16) If we live right we are always praising God. When we turn aside from justice and from all that pleases God then we cease to pray. So if you live right, "Though your tongue be silent, your life is eloquent and the ear of God is open to your heart." (Ps. 148,2)

Saint Augustine also commented on the words, "When the Son of Man comes, will he find, do you think, faith on the earth?" in conjunction with praying always. He tells us that to pray we must believe. "If faith fails, prayer dies." (PL 38, *Sermon 115*) Also, to stay firm in our faith we must pray. He sums both up by saying, "That we may pray, let us believe. And that the faith by which we pray may not fail, let us pray. Faith pours forth in prayer. And the prayer of faith poured forth obtains for us firmness in faith."

Another way of praying comes down to us from the Eastern tradition. The idea of praying a prayer repeatedly until it became habitual was popularized there by a possibly fictitious story called "The Way of the

Pilgrim." It was about a pilgrim who searched for a way to pray continuously. He met a hermit who taught him the "Jesus Prayer". The pilgrim prayed it a thousand times a day. Then the hermit had him pray it twelve thousand times a day. Finally, the prayer continued habitually in his heart.

"Pray always and do not lose heart." This has been the constant struggle of Christians throughout the centuries who wished to put Our Lord's words into practice. The struggle continues for us today. "For man it is impossible but with God all things are possible."

Thus the best, finest and fullest way of living is keeping in constant contact with God. Do it slowly. Move into this way through a process of practiced living that is both understandable and practical. You will become increasingly focused, increasingly centered. More and more we find ourselves going through the stresses and strains of daily activity with an ease and serenity that amaze us.

This should truly be the 'unbroken communion.'

The Apostle Paul described the need; "Pray without ceasing." (1Thes 5:17), "Rejoicing in hope; patient in tribulation; continuing instant in prayer;" (Rom 12:12), "Praying always with all prayer and supplication in the Spirit, and watching thereunto with all perseverance and supplication for all saints;" (Eph 6:18), "Continue in prayer, and watch in the same with thanksgiving;" (Col 4:2), "Be careful for nothing; but in every thing by prayer and supplication with thanksgiving let your requests be made known unto God." (Phil 4:6), "By him therefore let us offer the sacrifice of praise to God continually, that is, the fruit of our lips giving thanks to his name." (Heb 13:15)

Jesus also described the need, "And he spake a parable unto them to this end, that men ought always to pray, and not to faint;" (Luke 18:1). As well as modeling the need; "Then answered Jesus and said unto them, Verily, verily, I say unto you, The Son can do nothing of himself, but what he seeth the Father do: for what things soever he doeth, these also doeth the Son likewise." (John 5:19), "I can of mine own self do nothing: as I hear, I judge: and my judgment is just; because I seek not mine own will, but the will of the Father which hath sent me." (John 5:30) "I am the true vine, and my Father is the husbandman. Every branch in me that beareth not fruit he taketh away: and every branch that beareth fruit, he purgeth it, that it may bring forth more fruit. Now ye are clean through the word which I have spoken unto you. Abide in me, and I in you. As the branch cannot bear fruit of itself, except it abide in the vine; no more can ye, except ye abide in me. I am the vine, ye are the branches: He that abideth in me, and I in him, the same bringeth forth much fruit: for without me ye can do nothing. If a man abide not in me, he is cast forth as a branch, and is withered; and men gather them, and cast them into the fire, and they are burned. If ye abide in me, and my words abide in you, ye shall ask what ye will, and it shall be done unto you. Herein is my Father glorified, that ye bear much fruit; so shall ye be my disciples. As the Father hath loved me, so have I loved you: continue ye in my love. If ye keep my commandments, ye shall abide in my love; even as I have kept my Father's commandments, and abide in his love. These things have I spoken unto you, that my joy might remain in you, and that your joy might be full." (John 15:1-11)

Unceasing Prayer has a way of speaking peace to the chaos. We begin experiencing something of the cosmic patience of God. But this does not come automatically. We must want it, want it with a consuming passion.

Two Methods

The Breath Prayer

This method of prayer has it's origin in the Eastern Christian Hesychastic tradition and is usually called aspiratory prayer or breath prayer. The idea has its root in the Psalms, where a repeated phrase reminds us of an entire Psalm...Ps 139:1 *O LORD, thou hast searched me, and known me.*

The most famous of such prayers developed from the statement of the tax collector in Luke: "And the publican, standing afar off, would not lift up so much as his eyes unto heaven, but smote upon his breast, saying, God be merciful to me a sinner. It became "Lord, Jesus Christ, Son of God, have mercy on me, a sinner." (Luke 18:13) It came together in its present form and was used extensively in the sixth century and then was revived in the Eastern Church in the fourteenth century.

But, you can develop your own breath prayer.......to follow your own experiences and soul. You will find that you address our Lord in a very close and personal manner. You will also notice that you will develop a loving trust and comfort being in the Presence of God...you are slowly diminishing your own self-reliance, or ego...it does not focus on the individual but on God.

Practice of the Presence of God

This is a simple practice of going through the day in joyful awareness of God's presence with whispered prayers of praise and adoration flowing continuously from our hearts. This flows from an ordering of mental life on more than one level at once...we may continuously be in a "sense" of prayer while completing multiple practical tasks.

The procedural steps to this method are listed below. Review each and jot down any notes to yourself below each item.

1. Outward discipline. Pick a "trigger" that occurs manifold in your day to "remind" you to a call to prayer....washing dishes, cleaning the house, and yes, taking out the garbage. You can begin with this "game"...but it will quickly develop into habit.

Your note:

2. Move into the subconscious mind. With a continuation of "1" you will notice prayer bubbling into your mind at other times…..on a walk, in the shower, while taking your child to a soccer game, while babysitting your granddaughter.

Your note:

3. Prayer moves into the heart. Sentiment and reason act in concert. We find that our prayer becomes more spontaneous, open and "pure." You will be "prepared" by our Lord to sense the needs of others … as prayer is the open door to heaven which you now frequent. Be prepared to accept the call of our Lord to help others as a new gift provided "Deep calleth unto deep ……" (Ps 42:7)

Your note:

4. Prayer now permeates your entire personality

Your note:

Stop all that you are doing, and relax. Still your body and your mind. Seek to be at peace Know that you are in God's presence and that He encompasses you. Say this ancient Celtic prayer slowly, as you breathe in a normal relaxed fashion…remember, our Lord and Savior is present and stands next to you at this moment:

> *God to enfold me,*
> *God to surround me,*
> *God in my speaking,*
> *God in my thinking.*

God in my sleeping,
God in my waking,
God in my watching,
God in my hoping.

God in my life,
God in my lips,
God in my soul,
God in my heart.

God in my sufficing,
God in my slumber,
God in mine ever-lining soul,
God in mine eternity.
    (*Carmina Gadelica,* Volume III, pg 53)

Promise this week you will set aside time to be quiet, to be aware. Promise to pray in God's presence and to seek His will.

Say quietly and often… **"*I will go, Lord! Send me!*"**

Covenantal Prayer

Christian prayer is truly a *covenant relationship* between God and man in Christ. It is the action of God and of man, springing forth from both the Holy Spirit and ourselves, wholly directed through Jesus Christ to the Father, in union with the human will of the Son of God made man.

"Prayers are those by which we offer or vow something to God…""I will pay my vows unto the LORD now in the presence of all his people." (Ps 116:14) Where according to the exact force of the words it may be thus represented: "I will pay my prayers unto the Lord." "When thou vowest a vow unto God, defer not to pay it; for he hath no pleasure in fools: pay that which thou hast vowed. (Eccl 5:4) *It is better not to vow, than to vow and not to pay* (emphasis this author) which can be rendered in accordance with the Greek: It is better for thee not to pray than to pray and not to pay. "Better is it that thou shouldest not vow, than that thou shouldest vow and not pay." (Eccl 5:5)

Let us then not be at all cast down by despair from the confidence of this faith of ours, even when we fancy that we are far from having obtained what we prayed for, and let us not have any doubts about the Lord's promise where He says, "And all things, whatsoever ye shall ask in prayer, believing, ye shall receive." (Matt 21:22) He bids us then have a full and undoubting confidence of the answer only in those things which are not for our own advantage or for temporal comforts, but are in conformity to the Lord's will.

Cassian's Conferences, The First Conference of Abbot Isaac on Prayer, Chapter XII & XXXIV, AD495

Covenantal prayer is a profound interior heart call to a God-immersed life. It calls us to *commitment* and to a *path of holy obedience.* Such a call is not to be taken lightly. We find that the word covenant is used 271 times in Holy Scripture; certainly an indication of it's importance to you and to me.

God provided the example for us as he placed his covenant with the people as described in the Old Testament. These are *words of power, words of command, words of true love* for His creatures giving freedom but requiring discipline. "And God said, "This is the sign of the covenant I am making between me and you and every living creature with you, a covenant for all generations to come:" (Gen 9:12) "I have set my rainbow in the clouds, and it will be the sign of the covenant between me and the earth." (Gen 9:13) "I will remember my covenant between me and you and all living creatures of every kind…." (Gen 9:15)

Our Lord clearly states that *He will carry out his part of the Faithful combining* once made. Here he provides the words of assurance as He speaks to Abraham. "will confirm my covenant between me and you and will greatly increase your numbers." (Gen 17:2)

Discipline and commitment = freedom, and not the other way around. Once a covenant is made between you and the Lord, He will Faithfully commit to you But, "woe to thee who would cast aside such a relationship once made."

"And if you reject my decrees and abhor my laws and fail to carry out all my commands and so violate my covenant, then I will do this to you: I will bring upon you sudden terror, wasting diseases and fever that will destroy your sight and drain away your life. You will plant seed in vain, because your enemies will eat it. I will set my face against you so that you will be defeated by your enemies; those who hate you will rule over you, and you will flee even when no one is pursuing you. "'If after all this you will not listen to me, I will punish you for your sins seven times over. I will break down your stubborn pride and make the sky above you like iron and the ground beneath you like bronze. Your strength will be spent in vain, because your soil will not yield its crops, nor will the trees of the land yield their fruit. "'If you remain hostile toward me and refuse to listen to me, I will multiply your afflictions seven times over, as your sins deserve. I will send wild animals against you, and they will rob you of your children, destroy your cattle and make you so few in number that your roads will be deserted. "'If in spite of these things you do not accept my correction but continue to be hostile toward me, I myself will be hostile toward you and will afflict you for your sins seven times over...... "'If in spite of this you still do not listen to me but continue to be hostile toward me, then in my anger I will be hostile toward you, and I myself will punish you for your sins seven times over. You will eat the flesh of your sons and the flesh of your daughters. I will destroy your high places, cut down your incense altars and pile your dead bodies on the lifeless forms of your idols.. (Lev 26:15-30)

But for those who are faithful, "Now if you obey me fully and keep my covenant, then out of all nations you will be my treasured possession" (Exod 19:5)

And, even for those who are repentant about breaking a covenant, obtain the Sacrament of Reconciliation, and renew their covenant. "'But if they will confess their sins and the sins of their fathers—their treachery against me and their hostility toward me, which made me hostile toward them so that I sent them into the land of their enemies—then when their uncircumcised hearts are humbled and they pay for their sin, I will remember my covenant with Jacob and my covenant with Isaac and my covenant with Abraham, and I will remember the land." (Lev 26:40-42)

We must understand that our Lord requires us to obey once we enter a relationship with Him. We must not play at religion but rather we must LIVE our Religion. We also must understand that our Lord, through His Son, provided us the means to assure our Salvation in and through the Covenant of the Sacraments as described in the New Testament "This is my blood of the covenant, which is poured out for many for the forgiveness of sins." (Matt 26:28)

We are indeed blessed!! But we must still obey in the form of the Old Testament.

> "In the same way, after supper he took the cup, saying, "This cup is the new covenant in my blood; do this, whenever you drink it, in remembrance of me." For whenever you eat this bread and drink this cup, you proclaim the Lord's death until he comes. Therefore, whoever eats the bread or drinks the cup of the Lord in an unworthy manner will be guilty of sinning against the body and blood of the Lord. A man ought to examine himself before he eats of the bread and drinks of the cup. For anyone who eats and drinks without recognizing the body of the Lord eats and drinks judgment on himself." (1Cor 11:25-29)

Our New Covenant is now with Jesus Christ, with His teachings and the Salvation brought through His death.

> "He has made us competent as ministers of a new covenant—not of the letter but of the Spirit; for the letter kills, but the Spirit gives life." (2Cor 3:6)

> "But their minds were made dull, for to this day the same veil remains when the old covenant is read. It has not been

removed, because only in Christ is it taken away. Even to this day when Moses is read, a veil covers their hearts. But whenever anyone turns to the Lord, the veil is taken away. Now the Lord is the Spirit, and where the Spirit of the Lord is, there is freedom. And we, who with unveiled faces all reflect the Lord's glory, are being transformed into his likeness with ever-increasing glory, which comes from the Lord, who is the Spirit." (2Cor 3:14-18)

These are words of the New Testament describing the covenantal relationship remain words *of power, words of command, words of true love* for His creatures giving freedom but requiring discipline.

When it comes to prayer, we do not want to feel duty bound. We want to pray, as we feel drawn to it. We fear that commitments will make prayer seem like compulsory exercises rather tan free-will offerings. No, when undertaken in the power of the Spirit, *acts of duty can be filled with great joy and blessing*. In fact, duty is...."the sacrament of the present moment." (de Caussade).

We also shy away because of the fear that we cannot fulfill our covenant. But "Remember that God knows your heart...and bypasses your words. Promises rightly made are not forsaken." (John 13:36-38).

Life Giving Covenants: The purpose of a covenant is a commitment. Calvary's sacrifice is God's binding commitment. He has made covenant with us. Commitment demands commitment. What is our response? Are we willing to offer up lives of obedience in return?

Of Holy Obedience: Without reservation we vow to follow the Father......But, thank God, the matter of obedience is God's business and not ours. We cannot do a single good act except God first gives us the desire for it and then empowers us to do it. We do not have a burden here....but rather a love story with our God. God, you see, rushes to us at the first hint of our openness. You WILL feel waves of this love rush over you, OR an indescribable peace that will bring you to wordless adoration and submission to the wonder and glory. And you will be forever changed....*but you must have courage to face these times*. But it is also true that some of us will not experience either as described...and yet... be inextricably drawn to the heart of Jesus in small, continuing, warming, loving steps. When we fall down, we simply get up and continue our journey for once you taste this obedience you WILL desire to continue on the path to His glory.

We must seek out specifics
- Fittest time for prayer
- Fittest place for prayer
- Fittest preparation of heart for prayer

Of Time: A regular experience of prayer. This (as with Benedicts rule) will defeat self-importance and the wiles of the devil. The ancient Hebrew pattern was three times a day....later western traditions moved to seven times per day...but your patterns, family composition, job demands will require a unique answer for you. But once this is accomplished, we must firmly discipline ourselves to a regular schedule. Do not be tyrannized by the imagined urgent.

Of Place: Calls us to constancy...to be anchored somewhere. We must find "a place of focus"...from a garden to a simple chair if needs be. This also includes a commitment to community.

Of Heart Preparation: We can cultivate "holy expectancy." Control the tongue. Read sections of the great "prayer book of the Bible" the Psalms. Read prepatory prayers in the Common Book of Prayer or ancillary texts. Write and read your own words.

As in the writings of Ignatius Loyola, *The Spiritual Exercises*, there are four basic sections to your prayer
- Focus upon our sins in the light of God's Love
- Center on the life of Christ

- Focus on the passion of Christ
- Center on the resurrection of Christ

Then, and only then, you will find the words to speak a covenant with our Lord. Do not attempt to create a list from your mind, but from your Heart. It is at these moments that our Lord reveals the Covenant

There is not a specific form to the Covenantal prayer. It may be but two or three sentences in length. It may be several paragraphs. It may come to you in one session…but then again….it may come to you after a longer period of preparation.

The important element is this…it is THE prayer where our Lord speaks to you and to you only. It is THE relationship that he asks you to accept, to respond and to obey. It is THE path to salvation that he whispers in your ear as you draw near to his heart. "This is the covenant I will make with them after that time, says the Lord. I will put my laws in their hearts, and I will write them on their minds." (Heb 10:16)

May the love of our Lord fill your heart; may your spirit embrace the Living God such that your words and actions become "written in the heavens."

Part Four:

Prayer Exercises

Preparation for the Exercises

As you begin your journey towards a new and more fruitful prayer life there are certain guideposts that will prove very beneficial to your trip. Here we include the best fruits of spiritual exercises proposed by St. Ignatius Loyola, Joseph A. Fitzmeyer, S.J., the Ante Nicean, Nicean and Post Nicean Fathers of the Church and a number of authors. If you read this material during a prayer retreat, it would be wise to follow all of the instructions of your leader and this text to assure that you are familiar with those techniques proven to be useful. If you read this text in the privacy of your home allow me to suggest that you find as many opportunities as possible to include the instructions in their present format.

The exercises also assume that you executed a heart-centered confession and reconciliation followed by a penitent's Eucharist. This is absolutely essential. If you have not done this then STOP. Either participate in a prayer retreat where this essential preparation is included or contact your parish priest to perform a private confession just previous to a scheduled Mass (although you should include a penitent's confession and reconciliation prayers described earlier in this book).

Let us begin.

Your daily tasks: **particular examination of conscience (performed at three different times, and there are two examinations to be made)**

1. The first time: immediately upon getting up in the morning. Resolve to guard yourself carefully against the particular sin or defect that you wish to correct or amend.
2. The second time: after the noon meal you will ask God our Lord for what you desire, namely, the grace to remember how many times you have fallen into the particular sin or defect, and to correct yourself in the future.

Make the first examination demanding an account of your soul regarding that particular matter which you proposed for yourself and which you desire to correct and amend. Resolve to improve yourself until the time of the second examination.

Each time that one falls into the particular sin or defect, he should place his hand to his breast, representing that he has fallen

3. The third time: After the evening meal you will make a second examination, reviewing each hour from the first examination to this second one, and you will note each time that he has fallen into the particular sin or defect. Compare the second day with the first and one week to another.

Preparation for the individual exercises

Method of making the general examination of conscience
- Render thanks to God for the favors we have received
- Ask the grace to know my sins and to free myself from them
- Demand an account of my soul from the moment of rising until the present examination
- Ask pardon of God our Lord for my failings
- Resolve to amend my life with the help of God's grace. Close with the 'Our Father.'

Here we will proceed with the confession / reconciliation prayers described earlier in this text and receive Holy Communion

The First Prayer Exercise: A Person Beginning Serious Prayer

It is from the beginner's hopes and attitudes that the processes of spiritual growth develop.

- It is because you desire greater reflection and that you possess a faith-dimension that you decided on a greater pursuit of prayer.
- You have made a decision, not to begin something, but to live it more fully.
- At first there is a great deal to say…and you should say it. This will show your relationship to your Lord…and why he now makes this move in your life.
- Read the passages below, read thoroughly and allow the Scripture to speak directly to you, your life, your sinfulness and your desire to mature in your life with Christ. As you regularly use this text and re-read the readings below you will find that the Holy Spirit will speak to you in different ways each time, although the readings remain the same…that is important for your understanding of what is taking place in your spiritual life.
- A question of what is now happening in your current prayer life. You will need to develop a new language. After reading the selections below jot down your answers to the following questions.

❖ What happened?

❖ Which of those passages had the most to say to you?

❖ What struck you about it?

❖ How did you react?

❖ How will you react to correct your failings?

You will become more and more comfortable with this process over time, including your ability to talk about your findings!

Readings for the preliminary time of participants

First Reading (Ps 145:1-21)
"I will extol thee, my God, O king; and I will bless thy name for ever and ever. Every day will I bless thee; and I will praise thy name for ever and ever. Great is the LORD, and greatly to be praised; and his greatness is unsearchable. One generation shall praise thy works to another, and shall declare thy mighty acts. I will speak of the glorious honour of thy majesty, and of thy wondrous works. And men shall speak of the might of thy terrible acts: and I will declare thy greatness. They shall abundantly utter the memory of thy great goodness, and shall sing of thy righteousness. The LORD is gracious, and full of compassion; slow to anger, and of great mercy. The LORD is good to all: and his tender mercies are over all his works. All thy

works shall praise thee, O LORD; and thy saints shall bless thee. They shall speak of the glory of thy kingdom, and talk of thy power; To make known to the sons of men his mighty acts, and the glorious majesty of his kingdom. Thy kingdom is an everlasting kingdom, and thy dominion endureth throughout all generations. The LORD upholdeth all that fall, and raiseth up all those that be bowed down. The eyes of all wait upon thee; and thou givest them their meat in due season. Thou openest thine hand, and satisfiest the desire of every living thing. The LORD is righteous in all his ways, and holy in all his works. The LORD is nigh unto all them that call upon him, to all that call upon him in truth. He will fulfil the desire of them that fear him: he also will hear their cry, and will save them. The LORD preserveth all them that love him: but all the wicked will he destroy. My mouth shall speak the praise of the LORD: and let all flesh bless his holy name for ever and ever."

Second Reading (Ps 104:1-35)

"Bless the LORD, O my soul. O LORD my God, thou art very great; thou art clothed with honour and majesty. Who coverest thyself with light as with a garment: who stretchest out the heavens like a curtain: Who layeth the beams of his chambers in the waters: who maketh the clouds his chariot: who walketh upon the wings of the wind: Who maketh his angels spirits; his ministers a flaming fire: Who laid the foundations of the earth, that it should not be removed for ever. Thou coveredst it with the deep as with a garment: the waters stood above the mountains. At thy rebuke they fled; at the voice of thy thunder they hasted away. They go up by the mountains; they go down by the valleys unto the place which thou hast founded for them. Thou hast set a bound that they may not pass over; that they turn not again to cover the earth. He sendeth the springs into the valleys, which run among the hills. They give drink to every beast of the field: the wild asses quench their thirst. By them shall the fowls of the heaven have their habitation, which sing among the branches. He watereth the hills from his chambers: the earth is satisfied with the fruit of thy works. He causeth the grass to grow for the cattle, and herb for the service of man: that he may bring forth food out of the earth; And wine that maketh glad the heart of man, and oil to make his face to shine, and bread which strengtheneth man's heart. The trees of the LORD are full of sap; the cedars of Lebanon, which he hath planted; Where the birds make their nests: as for the stork, the fir trees are her house. The high hills are a refuge for the wild goats; and the rocks for the conies. He appointed the moon for seasons: the sun knoweth his going down. Thou makest darkness, and it is night: wherein all the beasts of the forest do creep forth. The young lions roar after their prey, and seek their meat from God. The sun ariseth, they gather themselves together, and lay them down in their dens. Man goeth forth unto his work and to his labour until the evening. O LORD, how manifold are thy works! in wisdom hast thou made them all: the earth is full of thy riches. So is this great and wide sea, wherein are things creeping innumerable, both small and great beasts. There go the ships: there is that leviathan, whom thou hast made to play therein. These wait all upon thee; that thou mayest give them their meat in due season. That thou givest them they gather: thou openest thine hand, they are filled with good. Thou hidest thy face, they are troubled: thou takest away their breath, they die, and return to their dust. Thou sendest forth thy spirit, they are created: and thou renewest the face of the earth. The glory of the LORD shall endure for ever: the LORD shall rejoice in his works. He looketh on the earth, and it trembleth: he toucheth the hills, and they smoke. I will sing unto the LORD as long as I live: I will sing praise to my God while I have my being. My meditation of him shall be sweet: I will be glad in the LORD. Let the sinners be consumed out of the earth, and let the wicked be no more. Bless thou the LORD, O my soul. Praise ye the LORD."

Third Reading (Ps 33:1-22)
"Rejoice in the LORD, O ye righteous: for praise is comely for the upright. Praise the LORD with harp: sing unto him with the psaltery and an instrument of ten strings. Sing unto him a new song; play skilfully with a loud noise. For the word of the LORD is right; and all his works are done in truth. He loveth righteousness and judgment: the earth is full of the goodness of the LORD. By the word of the LORD were the heavens made; and all the host of them by the breath of his mouth. He gathereth the waters of the sea together as an heap: he layeth up the depth in storehouses. Let all the earth fear the LORD: let all the inhabitants of the world stand in awe of him. For he spake, and it was done; he commanded, and it stood fast. The LORD bringeth the counsel of the heathen to nought: he maketh the devices of the people of none effect. The counsel of the LORD standeth for ever, the thoughts of his heart to all generations. Blessed is the nation whose God is the LORD; and the people whom he hath chosen for his own inheritance. The LORD looketh from heaven; he beholdeth all the sons of men. From the place of his habitation he looketh upon all the inhabitants of the earth. He fashioneth their hearts alike; he considereth all their works. There is no king saved by the multitude of an host: a mighty man is not delivered by much strength. An horse is a vain thing for safety: neither shall he deliver any by his great strength. Behold, the eye of the

LORD is upon them that fear him, upon them that hope in his mercy; To deliver their soul from death, and to keep them alive in famine. Our soul waiteth for the LORD: he is our help and our shield. For our heart shall rejoice in him, because we have trusted in his holy name. Let thy mercy, O LORD, be upon us, according as we hope in thee."

Fourth Reading (Ps 112:1-10)

"Praise ye the LORD. Blessed is the man that feareth the LORD, that delighteth greatly in his commandments. His seed shall be mighty upon earth: the generation of the upright shall be blessed. Wealth and riches shall be in his house: and his righteousness endureth for ever. Unto the upright there ariseth light in the darkness: he is gracious, and full of compassion, and righteous. A good man sheweth favour, and lendeth: he will guide his affairs with discretion. Surely he shall not be moved for ever: the righteous shall be in everlasting remembrance. He shall not be afraid of evil tidings: his heart is fixed, trusting in the LORD. His heart is established, he shall not be afraid, until he see his desire upon his enemies.

He hath dispersed, he hath given to the poor; his righteousness endureth for ever; his horn shall be exalted with honour. The wicked shall see it, and be grieved; he shall gnash with his teeth, and melt away: the desire of the wicked shall perish."

The Second Prayer Exercise: Confession or Lamentation Period

The second prayer exercise is somewhat similar to the first but here we consider our sins more deeply. To weigh your sins, considering the loathsomeness and the malice that every sin committed has in itself, even though it were not forbidden.

Let us read the following preludes very carefully...as if your soul depended upon understanding them!

> *The First Prelude:*
> Our Lord descending with his eleven disciples from Mount Sion, where the Supper was held, to the Valley of Josaphat. Leaving the eight in one part of the valley, He took the other three apart into the Garden. He then began to pray and His sweat became drops of blood. After the events of the garden He was led through the valley and back up to slope to the House of Annas and eventually to Pilot.

> *The Second Prelude:*
> Visualize the movement of Christ from the house of Pilate to the horrible treatment with the scourging and crown of thorns, passing through the walkways of the city to the place of the skull, Golgatha. Visualize the period from the Last Supper

to the Crucifixion, the nailing to the cross, and from the raising of the cross to His death.

The Third Prelude:

Now you can see his limp and battered body being slowly lowered from the cross with the deep grieving of His mother and those attending to the burial in the sepulcher. Consider how the most Sacred Body of Christ our Lord remained separated and apart from His Soul, also where and how it was buried. Consider likewise the desolation of our Lady, her great grief and weariness, also that of the disciples. Consider your presence with His Mother, consider your consolation of her, your arm around her, your words with her....a mother who has lost a son in a most horrible manner.

As in the first exercise, read the passages below, read thoroughly and allow the Scripture to speak directly to you, your life, your sinfulness and your desire to mature in your life with Christ. As you regularly use this text and re-read the readings below you will find that the Holy Spirit will speak to you in different ways each time, although the readings remain the same...that is important for your understanding of what is taking place in your spiritual life.

As in the first exercise, after reading the Scripture excerpts below, ask these questions and jot your answers down under each:

- Which of those passages had the most to say to you?

- What struck you about it?

- How did you react?

- How will you react to correct your failings?

Now, after considering the above infused with the Scripture readings, continue on and consider "who I am"
- What am I in comparison to all men?
- What are men in comparison with the angels and saints of heaven?

- What is all creation in comparison with God? The myself alone, what can it be?
- Let me consider all my own corruption and foulness of body
- Let me see myself as a source of so many sins, so many evils.

Now compare how contrary the nature of God is to your actions.

- Make a plea to Jesus Christ.   A complaint that God should correct a skewed situation
- Make your address to Jesus.   Intimate and personal. A stranger to Yahweh does not speak the complaint, but one who has a long history of trustful interaction.
- Complaint.   Characterize for Jesus how desperate the situation is. Characterizing the depth of the problem...in all possible terms.
- Petition.   Make a petition that asks Jesus to act decisively. Clear wording asks for attentive compassion...and speaks to his opportunity through Scripture. A plea for justice as much as mercy.
- Now consider the amazing truths. How the angels, the swords of Divine Justice, tolerated you, guarded you, and prayed for you. How the saints have interceded and prayed for you. How the elements created by God have all served your needs. How the earth has not opened and swallowed you up to suffer justice for my sins.

Readings for Prayer Process 2

First Reading (Ps 13:1-6)

"How long wilt thou forget me, O LORD? for ever? how long wilt thou hide thy face from me? How long shall I take counsel in my soul, having sorrow in my heart daily? how long shall mine enemy be exalted over me?

Consider and hear me, O LORD my God: lighten mine eyes, lest I sleep the sleep of death; Lest mine enemy say, I have prevailed against him; and those that trouble me rejoice when I am moved. But I have trusted in thy mercy; my heart shall rejoice in thy salvation. I will sing unto the LORD, because he hath dealt bountifully with me.

Second Reading (Ps 86:1-17)
"Bow down thine ear, O LORD, hear me: for I am poor and needy. Preserve my soul; for I am holy: O thou my God, save thy servant that trusteth in thee. Be merciful unto me, O Lord: for I cry unto thee daily.

Rejoice the soul of thy servant: for unto thee, O Lord, do I lift up my soul.

For thou, Lord, art good, and ready to forgive; and plenteous in mercy unto all them that call upon thee. Give ear, O LORD, unto my prayer; and attend to the voice of my supplications. In the day of my trouble I will call upon thee: for thou wilt answer me. Among the gods there is none like unto thee, O Lord; neither are there any works like unto thy works. All nations whom thou hast made shall come and worship before thee, O Lord; and shall glorify thy name. For thou art great, and doest wondrous things: thou art God alone. Teach me thy way, O LORD; I will walk in thy truth: unite my heart to fear thy name. I will praise thee, O Lord my God, with all my heart: and I will glorify thy name for evermore. For great is thy mercy toward me: and thou hast delivered my soul from the lowest hell. O God, the proud are risen against me, and the assemblies of violent men have sought after my soul; and have not set thee before them. But thou, O Lord, art a God full of compassion, and gracious, longsuffering, and plenteous in mercy and truth. O turn unto me, and have mercy upon me; give thy strength unto thy servant, and save the son of thine handmaid. Shew me a token for good; that they which hate me may see it, and be ashamed: because thou, LORD, hast holpen me, and comforted me."

Third Reading (Ps 35:1-28)

"Plead my cause, O LORD, with them that strive with me: fight against them that fight against me. Take hold of shield and buckler, and stand up for mine help. Draw out also the spear, and stop the way against them that persecute me: say unto my soul, I am thy salvation. Let them be confounded and put to shame that seek after my soul: let them be turned back and brought to confusion that devise my hurt. Let them be as chaff before the wind: and let the angel of the LORD chase them. Let their way be dark and slippery: and let the angel of the LORD persecute them. For without cause have they hid for me their net in a pit, which without cause they have digged for my soul. Let destruction come upon him at unawares; and let his net that he hath hid catch himself: into that very destruction let him fall. And my soul shall be joyful in the LORD: it shall rejoice in his salvation. All my bones shall say, LORD, who is like unto thee, which deliverest the poor from him that is too strong for him, yea, the poor and the needy from him that spoileth him? False witnesses did rise up; they laid to my charge things that I knew not. They rewarded me evil for good to the spoiling of my soul. But as for me, when they were sick, my clothing was sackcloth: I humbled my soul with fasting; and my prayer returned into mine own bosom. I behaved myself as though he had been my friend or brother: I bowed down heavily, as one that mourneth for his mother. But in mine adversity they rejoiced, and gathered themselves together: yea, the abjects gathered themselves together against me, and I knew it not; they did tear me, and ceased not: With hypocritical mockers in feasts, they gnashed upon me with their teeth. Lord, how long wilt thou look on? rescue my soul from their destructions, my darling from the lions. I will give thee thanks in the great congregation: I will praise thee among much people. Let not them that are mine enemies wrongfully rejoice over me: neither let them wink with the eye that hate me without a cause. For they speak not peace: but they devise deceitful matters against them that are quiet in the land. Yea, they opened their mouth wide against me, and said, Aha, aha, our eye hath seen it. This thou hast seen, O LORD: keep not silence: O Lord, be not far from me. Stir up thyself, and awake to my judgment, even unto my cause, my God and my Lord. Judge me, O LORD my God, according to thy righteousness; and let them not rejoice over me. Let them not say in their hearts, Ah, so would we have it: let them not say, We have swallowed him up. Let them be ashamed and brought to confusion together that rejoice at mine hurt: let them be clothed with shame and dishonour that magnify themselves against me. Let them shout for joy, and be glad, that favour my righteous cause: yea, let them say continually, Let the LORD be magnified, which hath pleasure in the prosperity of his servant. And my tongue shall speak of thy righteousness and of thy praise all the day long."

Fourth Reading (John 19:1-11)

"Then Pilate therefore took Jesus, and scourged him. And the soldiers platted a crown of thorns, and put it on his head, and they put on him a purple robe, And said, Hail, King of the Jews! and they smote him with their hands. Pilate therefore went forth again, and saith unto them, Behold, I bring him forth to you, that ye may know that I find no fault in him.

Then came Jesus forth, wearing the crown of thorns, and the purple robe. And Pilate saith unto them, Behold the man! When the chief priests therefore and officers saw him, they cried out, saying, Crucify him, crucify him. Pilate saith unto them, Take ye him, and crucify him: for I find no fault in him. The Jews answered him, We have a law, and by our law he ought to die, because he made himself the Son of God. When Pilate therefore heard that saying, he was the more afraid; And went again into the judgment hall, and saith unto Jesus, Whence art thou? But Jesus gave him no answer. Then saith Pilate unto him, Speakest thou not unto me? knowest thou not that I have power to crucify thee, and have power to release thee? Jesus answered, Thou couldest have no power at all against me, except it were given thee from above: therefore he that delivered me unto thee hath the greater sin."

Fifth Reading (John 19:12-24)

"And from thenceforth Pilate sought to release him: but the Jews cried out, saying, If thou let this man go, thou art not Caesar's friend: whosoever maketh himself a king speaketh against Caesar. When Pilate therefore heard that saying, he brought Jesus forth, and sat down in the judgment seat in a place that is called the Pavement, but in the Hebrew, Gabbatha.

And it was the preparation of the passover, and about the sixth hour: and he saith unto the Jews, Behold your King! But they cried out, Away with him, away with him, crucify him. Pilate saith unto them, Shall I crucify your King? The chief priests answered, We have no king but Caesar. Then delivered he him therefore unto them to be crucified. And they took Jesus, and led him away. And he bearing his cross went forth into a place called the place of a skull, which is called in the Hebrew Golgotha: Where they crucified him, and two other with him, on either side one, and Jesus in the midst. And Pilate wrote a title, and put it on the cross. And the writing was, JESUS OF NAZARETH THE KING OF THE JEWS. This title then read many of the Jews: for the place where Jesus was crucified was nigh to the city: and it was written in Hebrew, and Greek, and Latin. Then said the chief priests of the Jews to Pilate, Write not, The King of the Jews; but that he said, I am King of the Jews. Pilate answered, What I have written I have written. Then the soldiers, when they had crucified Jesus, took his garments, and made four parts, to every soldier a part; and also his coat: now the coat was without seam, woven from the top throughout. They said therefore among themselves, Let us not rend it, but cast lots for it, whose it shall be: that the scripture might be fulfilled, which saith, They parted my raiment among them, and for my vesture they did cast lots. These things therefore the soldiers did."

Sixth Reading (John 19:23-37)

"Then the soldiers, when they had crucified Jesus, took his garments, and made four parts, to every soldier a part; and also his coat: now the coat was without seam, woven from the top throughout. They said therefore among themselves, Let us not rend it, but cast lots for it, whose it shall be: that the scripture might be fulfilled, which saith, They parted my raiment among them, and for my vesture they did cast lots. These things therefore the soldiers did. Now there stood by the cross of Jesus his mother, and his mother's sister, Mary the wife of Cleophas, and

Mary Magdalene. When Jesus therefore saw his mother, and the disciple standing by, whom he loved, he saith unto his mother, Woman, behold thy son! Then saith he to the disciple, Behold thy mother! And from that hour that disciple took her unto his own home. After this, Jesus knowing that all things were now accomplished, that the scripture might be fulfilled, saith, I thirst. Now there was set a vessel full of vinegar: and they filled a spunge with vinegar, and put it upon hyssop, and put it to his mouth. When Jesus therefore had received the vinegar, he said, It is finished: and he bowed his head, and gave up the ghost. The Jews therefore, because it was the preparation, that the bodies should not remain upon the cross on the sabbath day, (for that sabbath day was an high day,) besought Pilate that their legs might be broken, and that they might be taken away. Then came the soldiers, and brake the legs of the first, and of the other which was crucified with him. But when they came to Jesus, and saw that he was dead already, they brake not his legs: But one of the soldiers with a spear pierced his side, and forthwith came there out blood and water. And he that saw it bare record, and his record is true: and he knoweth that he saith true, that ye might believe. For these things were done, that the scripture should be fulfilled, A bone of him shall not be broken. And again another scripture saith, They shall look on him whom they pierced."

Seventh Reading (Matt 27:35-39)

"And they crucified him, and parted his garments, casting lots: that it might be fulfilled which was spoken by the prophet, They parted my garments among them, and upon my vesture did they cast lots. And sitting down they watched him there; And set up over his head his accusation written, THIS IS

JESUS THE KING OF THE JEWS. Then were there two thieves crucified with him, one on the right hand, and another on the left. And they that passed by reviled him, wagging their heads,"

Eighth Reading (Mark 15:24-38)
"And when they had crucified him, they parted his garments, casting lots upon them, what every man should take. And it was the third hour, and they crucified him. And the superscription of his accusation was written over, THE KING OF THE JEWS. And with him they crucify two thieves; the one on his right hand, and the other on his left. And the scripture was fulfilled, which saith, And he was numbered with the transgressors. And they that passed by railed on him, wagging their heads, and saying, Ah, thou that destroyest the temple, and buildest it in three days, Save thyself, and come down from the cross. Likewise also the chief priests mocking said among themselves with the scribes, He saved others; himself he cannot save. Let Christ the King of Israel descend now from the cross, that we may see and believe. And they that were crucified with him reviled him. And when the sixth hour was come, there was darkness over the whole land until the ninth hour. And at the ninth hour Jesus cried with a loud voice, saying, Eloi, Eloi, lama sabachthani? which is, being interpreted, My God, my God, why hast thou forsaken me?   And some of them that stood by, when they heard it, said, Behold, he calleth Elias. And one ran and filled a spunge full of vinegar, and put it on a reed, and gave him to drink, saying, Let alone; let us see whether Elias will come to take him down. And Jesus cried with a loud voice, and gave up the ghost. And the veil of the temple was rent in twain from the top to the bottom."

Ninth Reading (Luke 23:34-46)

"Then said Jesus, Father, forgive them; for they know not what they do. And they parted his raiment, and cast lots. And the people stood beholding. And the rulers also with them derided him, saying, He saved others; let him save himself, if he be Christ, the chosen of God. And the soldiers also mocked him, coming to him, and offering him vinegar, And saying, If thou be the king of the Jews, save thyself. And a superscription also was written over him in letters of Greek, and Latin, and Hebrew, THIS IS THE KING OF THE JEWS. And one of the malefactors which were hanged railed on him, saying, If thou be Christ, save thyself and us. But the other answering rebuked him, saying, Dost not thou fear God, seeing thou art in the same condemnation? And we indeed justly; for we receive the due reward of our deeds: but this man hath done nothing amiss.

And he said unto Jesus, Lord, remember me when thou comest into thy kingdom. And Jesus said unto him, Verily I say unto thee, To day shalt thou be with me in paradise. And it was about the sixth hour, and there was a darkness over all the earth until the ninth hour. And the sun was darkened, and the veil of the temple was rent in the midst And when Jesus had cried with a loud voice, he said, Father, into thy hands I commend my spirit: and having said thus, he gave up the ghost."

The Third Prayer Exercise: The Final Phase of the Process

Things are different. Something has changed. The sense of urgency and desperation is replaced by joy, gratitude, and well-being.

First Prelude:

During this prelude consider the resurrection and the first through the thirteenth apparitions. Visualize the sepulcher. Visualize the space the rock formation the dirt floor and the stone against the entrance. See the body of our Lord move without corruption as His Soul rejoins His body. Now walk through the apparitions of our Lord to those who remain behind.

Second Prelude:

Visualize our Lord upon the rock, His glorious light-filled being. Here it is to see how I stand in the presence of God our Lord and the angels and the saints, who intercede for me.

Know that your sins are forgiven; they are bound to the suffering of our Lord and now the blessings flow to your heart and soul represented by His glorious resurrection and ascension into heaven. Here you ask for what you desire. Here it will be to ask for a deep knowledge of the many blessings I have received, that I may be filled with gratitude for them, and in all things love and serve the Divine Majesty.

I will ponder with great affection how much God our Lord has done for me, and how many of His graces He has given me. I will likewise consider how much the same Lord wishes to give Himself to me in so far as He can, according to His divine decrees.

I will consider how He dwells in me, giving life, sensation, intelligence, and being and making a temple of me, since He created me in the likeness and image of His Divine Majesty. All of my being comes from the supreme and infinite power from above. In like manner justice, goodness, pity, mercy and all other gifts descend from above just as the rays from the sun, the waters from the spring, etc.

I will now know that my sins are forgiven; that my gifts are shining within my heart and to the depths of my soul. God has touched me this day. I will put on the helmet of salvation and breastplate of righteousness. I am a new creation in His sight....to shine within my family, church and community.

Conclude with the 'Our Father.'

Know that your life is changing through Jesus Christ:

- Assurance of being heard. — *And therefore an action is possible.*
- Payment of vows. — *Praise as the obligation.*
- Doxology and praise. — *Generous and faithful and saving.*

As in the first and second exercises, after reading the Scripture excerpts below, ask these questions:

- Which of those passages had the most to say to you?

- What struck you about it?

- How did you react?

- How will you react to your new life in Jesus Christ?

Readings for Prayer Process 3

First Reading (Ps 30:1-12)

"I will extol thee, O LORD; for thou hast lifted me up, and hast not made my foes to rejoice over me. O LORD my God, I cried unto thee, and thou hast healed me. O LORD, thou hast brought up my soul from the grave: thou hast kept me alive, that I should not go down to the pit. Sing unto the LORD, O ye saints of his, and give thanks at the remembrance of his holiness. For his anger endureth but a moment; in his favour is life: weeping may endure for a night, but joy cometh in the morning. And in my prosperity I said, I shall never be moved. LORD, by thy favour thou hast made my mountain to stand strong: thou didst hide thy face, and I was troubled. I cried to thee, O LORD; and unto the LORD I made supplication. What profit is there in my blood, when I go down to the pit? Shall the dust praise thee? shall it declare thy truth?   Hear, O LORD, and have mercy upon me: LORD, be thou my helper. Thou hast turned for me my mourning into dancing: thou hast put off my sackcloth, and girded me with gladness; To the end that my glory may sing praise to thee, and not be silent. O LORD my God, I will give thanks unto thee for ever."

Second Reading (Ps 40:1-17)

I waited patiently for the LORD; and he inclined unto me, and heard my cry. He brought me up also out of an horrible pit, out of the miry clay, and set my feet upon a rock, and established my goings. And he hath put a new song in my mouth, even praise unto our God: many shall see it, and fear, and shall trust in the LORD. Blessed is that man that maketh the LORD his trust, and respecteth not the proud, nor such as turn aside to lies. Many, O LORD my God, are thy wonderful works which thou hast done, and thy thoughts which are to usward: they cannot be reckoned up in order unto thee: if I would declare and speak of them, they are more than can be numbered. Sacrifice and offering thou didst not desire; mine ears hast thou opened: burnt offering and sin offering hast thou not required. Then said I, Lo, I come: in the volume of the book it is written of me, I delight to do thy will, O my God: yea, thy law is within my heart.

I have preached righteousness in the great congregation: lo, I have not refrained my lips, O LORD, thou knowest. I have not hid thy righteousness within my heart; I have declared thy faithfulness and thy salvation: I have not concealed thy lovingkindness and thy truth from the great congregation. Withhold not thou thy tender mercies from me, O LORD: let thy lovingkindness and thy truth continually preserve me. For innumerable evils have compassed me about: mine iniquities have taken hold upon me, so that I am not able to look up; they are more than the hairs of mine head: therefore my heart faileth me. Be pleased, O LORD, to deliver me: O LORD, make haste to help me. Let them be ashamed and confounded together that seek after my soul to destroy it; let them be driven backward and put to shame that wish me evil. Let them be desolate for a reward of their shame that say unto me, Aha, aha. Let all those that seek thee rejoice and be glad in thee: let such as love thy salvation say continually, The LORD be magnified. But I am poor and needy; yet the Lord thinketh upon me: thou art my help and my deliverer; make no tarrying, O my God.

Third Reading (Ps 34:1-22)

I will bless the LORD at all times: his praise shall continually be in my mouth. My soul shall make her boast in the LORD: the humble shall hear thereof, and be glad. O magnify the LORD with me, and let us exalt his name together. I sought the LORD, and he heard me, and delivered me from all my fears. They looked unto him, and were lightened: and their faces were not ashamed. This poor man cried, and the LORD heard him, and saved him out of all his troubles. The angel of the LORD encampeth round about them that fear him, and delivereth them. O taste and see that the LORD is good: blessed is the man that trusteth in him. O fear the LORD, ye his saints: for there is no want to them that fear him. The young lions do lack, and suffer hunger: but they that seek the LORD shall not want any good thing. Come, ye children, hearken unto me: I will teach you the fear of the LORD. What man is he that desireth life, and loveth many days, that he may see good? Keep thy tongue from evil, and thy lips from speaking guile. Depart from evil, and do good; seek peace, and pursue it. The eyes of the LORD are upon the righteous, and his ears are open unto their cry. The face of the LORD is against them that do evil, to cut off the remembrance of them from the earth. The righteous cry, and the LORD heareth, and delivereth them out of all their troubles. The LORD is nigh unto them that are of a broken heart; and saveth such as be of a contrite spirit. Many are the afflictions of the righteous: but the LORD delivereth him out of them all. He keepeth all his bones: not one of them is broken. Evil shall slay the wicked: and they that hate the righteous shall be desolate. The LORD redeemeth the soul of his servants: and none of them that trust in him shall be desolate.

Fourth Reading (Ps 138:1-8)

I will praise thee with my whole heart: before the gods will I sing praise unto thee. I will worship toward thy holy temple, and praise thy name for thy lovingkindness and for thy truth: for thou hast magnified thy word above all thy name. In the day when I cried thou answeredst me, and strengthenedst me with strength in my soul. All the kings of the earth shall praise thee, O LORD, when they hear the words of thy mouth. Yea, they shall sing in the ways of the LORD: for great is the glory of the LORD. Though the LORD be high, yet hath he respect unto the lowly: but the proud he knoweth afar off. Though I walk in the midst of trouble, thou wilt revive me: thou shalt stretch forth thine hand against the wrath of mine enemies, and thy right hand shall save me. The LORD will perfect that which concerneth me: thy mercy, O LORD, endureth for ever: forsake not the works of thine own hands.

Fifth Reading (Acts 1:1-11)

The former treatise have I made, O Theophilus, of all that Jesus began both to do and teach, Until the day in which he was taken up, after that he through the Holy Ghost had given commandments unto the apostles whom he had chosen: To whom also he shewed himself alive after his passion by many infallible proofs, being seen of them forty days, and speaking of the things pertaining to the kingdom of God: And, being assembled together with them, commanded them that they should not depart from Jerusalem, but wait for the promise of the Father, which, saith he, ye have heard of me. For John truly baptized with water; but ye shall be baptized with the Holy Ghost not many days hence. When they therefore were come together, they asked of him, saying, Lord, wilt thou at this time restore again the kingdom to Israel? And he said unto them, It is not for you to know the times or the seasons, which the Father hath put in his own power. But ye shall receive power, after that the Holy Ghost is come upon you: and ye shall be witnesses unto me both in Jerusalem, and in all Judaea, and in Samaria, and unto the uttermost part of the earth. And when he had spoken these things, while they beheld, he was taken up; and a cloud received him out of their sight. And while they looked stedfastly toward heaven as he went up, behold, two men stood by them in white apparel; Which also said, Ye men of Galilee, why stand ye gazing up into heaven? this same Jesus, which is taken up from you into heaven, shall so come in like manner as ye have seen him go into heaven.

Epilogue

"….the way ye know." (John 14:4)

Slán agus beannacht.
(Good Bye and Blessings)

Appendix One
Prayer Ministry: Anamchara (Prayer Mate)

Aiden of Lindesfarne, a Celtic monk originally from Iona, developed a wonderful and effective ministry throughout Northumbria. This included the development of a school as the primary focus of the Ministry of the Word. Upon entering the school each of the brothers took on a anamchara—a cell mate/prayer mate.. In the same way you are urged to take on a anamchara—a prayer mate/prayer partner, to continue your prayer journey with our Lord. As the anamchara of Aiden's time, you must also have a living faith, a faith that comes from your heart. Aiden would remind the Celtic monks again and again, *'You cannot bring about what you have not let be poured in.'* As a anamchara to another and they to you, your ability to grow in faith will increase exponentially... *"and dost promise that when two or three are gathered together in thy Name thou wilt grant their requests.."* *(A prayer of St. Chrysostom)* Together, you will learn the way of prayer and the miraculous benefits accorded to your faithfulness.

Here is how to do it!

Come together with one other individual. That person with whom you can pray intently, privately, intimately and deeply with our Lord, Jesus Christ. Together your can hold one-another accountable, pray the prayer of petition for your needs and the needs of your prayer partner and pray intercessory prayer on behalf of others.

The following can be used for your benefit.

- Come as a servant to one another and to Jesus Christ. Realize that your partner is not there to meet your needs and the prayer needs of your family. Although they pray for their partners, do not take advantage of them.
- When you talk to your partner on the phone, state what the Lord has given you quickly and concisely.
- Don't be offended if he/she doesn't speak to you in person (message machine). He/she may not be able to do so at the moment. This does not mean that he/she does not care. Just be very careful with the details that you leave in a voice message such that you or anyone else will not be embarrassed or offended if someone other than your anamchara listens to the messages first!
- Be careful about warning the person for whom you are praying that you are praying for them they may have too much to handle at the moment.
- If you believe that you have a premonition of something, always take it to the Lord first for an interpretation through your own prayers.
- It may take time to build trust in the validity of your ministry of intercession. Be faithful in your praying and the relationship will come.
- Remain conservative and quiet in your activities. This is a confidential trust.
- **Give your parish priest feedback on a regular basis on what the Lord is telling you and your experiences.**
- Pray for protection for your own family as you intercede. Pray the following every day in your daily prayers.

(Ps 91:1-16)

He that dwelleth in the secret place of the most High shall abide under the shadow of the Almighty. I will say of the LORD, He is my refuge and my fortress: my God; in him will I trust. Surely he shall deliver thee from the snare of the fowler, and from the noisome pestilence. He shall cover thee with his feathers, and under his wings shalt thou trust: his truth shall be thy shield and buckler. Thou shalt not be afraid for the terror by night; nor for the arrow that flieth by day; Nor for the pestilence that walketh in darkness; nor for the destruction that wasteth at noonday. A thousand shall fall at thy side, and ten thousand at thy right hand; but it shall not come nigh thee. Only with thine eyes shalt thou behold and see the reward of the wicked. Because thou hast made the LORD, which is my refuge, even the most High, thy habitation; There shall no evil befall thee, neither shall any plague come nigh thy dwelling. For he shall give his angels charge over thee, to keep thee in all thy ways. They shall bear thee up in their hands, lest thou dash thy foot against a stone. Thou shalt tread upon the lion and adder: the young lion and the dragon shalt thou trample under feet. Because he hath set his love upon me, therefore will I deliver him: I will set him on high, because he hath known my name. He shall call upon me, and I will answer him: I will be with him in trouble; I will deliver him, and honour him. With long life will I satisfy him, and shew him my salvation.

Appendix Two
Prayer Ministry: Prayer Groups

A ministry team is a group of three or more Christians who come together in love, representing the Body of Christ in ministering to a vulnerable member or members of His Family. The team is not just a group of individuals, but is a dedicated ministry led and fed by the Holy Spirit. By operating as a team, members with their different spiritual gifts, talents and personalities are able to make Jesus real to the person being prayed for. They are more than petitioners; they are being used by Christ as channels of His healing power to heal a member if His body.

Jesus recognized the need for ministry teams: He sent out His disciples in pairs for preaching and healing.

"Take heed that ye despise not one of these little ones; for I say unto you, That in heaven their angels do always behold the face of my Father which is in heaven. For the Son of man is come to save that which was lost. How think ye? if a man have an hundred sheep, and one of them be gone astray, doth he not leave the ninety and nine, and goeth into the mountains, and seeketh that which is gone astray? And if so be that he find it, verily I say unto you, he rejoiceth more of that sheep, than of the ninety and nine which went not astray. Even so it is not the will of your Father which is in heaven, that one of these little ones should perish. Moreover if thy brother shall trespass against thee, go and tell him his fault between thee and him alone: if he shall hear thee, thou hast gained thy brother. But if he will not hear thee, then take with thee one or two more, that in the mouth of two or three witnesses every word may be established. And if he shall neglect to hear them, tell it unto the church: but if he neglect to hear the church, let him be unto thee as an heathen man and a publican. Verily I say unto you, Whatsoever ye shall bind on earth shall be bound in heaven: and whatsoever ye shall loose on earth shall be loosed in heaven. Again I say unto you, That if two of you shall agree on earth as touching any thing that they shall ask, it shall be done for them of my Father which is in heaven. For where two or three are gathered together in my name, there am I in the midst of them." (Matt 18:10-20)

"He gave them power and authority to drive out all demons and to cure diseases, and he sent them out to preach the kingdom of God and to heal the sick." (Luke 9:1-2)

How to get started.
- Pray. The proper place to begin anything in the Church is in Prayer, and Prayer Ministries are no exception.
- Pray often, pray regularly, and pray with others who understand the need for prayer.

Obtain the support of your priest.
- No ministry within a parish is likely to survive without the genuine endorsement of the priest, and a prayer ministry is no exception.

Laity involvement and leadership
- Laity mutual support, the lack of dominance, and care for other team members (this is a stressful ministry if done well) are essential.
- The selection of a leader is very important and can be a critical turning point even before the ministry has begun. The person must have the gift of leadership. They should participate in a retreat and training such as that described in this text before participating in such an important venture.

Some practical tips

First, and most important, beware of the deceptions of Satan.
For all the reasons to start a prayer ministry, and for all the reasons we wish to pray more and better, and wish others to also pray, Satan will oppose us (read the *Screwtape Letters* by C.S. Lewis for a light-hearted discussion). You can rest assured that if you are making progress, he will increase his attempts to distract you. *It is absolutely necessary that you pray to Jesus for protection from his whiles.* That you pray for your family and those close to you. That you pray for others who are involved in building a prayer ministry. Prayer will cause Satan concern BECAUSE prayer is our best defense.

Second, do not underestimate the first point above!
Satan, by definition, cannot stop prayer, so he will attempt *to stop you* and those around you.

Third, don't organize Jesus out of your Ministry.
Leave room for God's hand in all that you do. If you wish to establish a prayer Ministry, then for heaven's sake, depend upon prayer as much as you do your agenda and Robert's Rules of Order!

Fourth, teach prayer.

When possible, allow for a prayer retreat. But you may also include a special get-together of parishioners at Adult Education, Scripture Study, etc. to inform them of your actions, attract those who believe they are drawn to such ministry and to gain the strength of their prayers as your group grows in its Ministry.

Don't start too many things at once or try to move too quickly.

Not everyone will participate in every given activity of the Ministry.

Not everything is right for everyone, in fact do not expect your prayer Ministry's inner-circle to participate in every activity. Do not expect your leaders to participate in everything. People, led by the Lord, must do what is right for them. Do not be surprised by who does or doesn't participate, but rejoice and thank the Lord for those he leads to participate.

Report all that you do to your parish priest or to the persons or committees that he designates for this purpose.

Respond when someone from the congregation tries to use a given activity in a way that you didn't anticipate.

A request applying to a prayer activity is a good indicator that you are succeeding with that person, if you can accommodate that person you should do so. The Lord can use our work to produce fruits that we have no understanding of, and never anticipated. After all, it is all for His Glory…and not ours!

Allow for a variety of commitment in your activities.

Much is written about the shift in the mentality of today's citizens. One trait consistently brought to the front, is that people are less willing to commit for long periods. Keep a mix of crucial activities. There are people who will make one commitment for one week 52 times in a row, but they would not consider making a commitment for a year to the same activity!

Understand that not all parishioners are at the same point of Spiritual maturity, and not all will grow at the same rate, or even with the same goals

A Prayer Ministry Model
(Based on Good Shepherd's Prayer Ministry)

The Prayer Support Group
- This is the inner circle or steering committee
- The group initially met weekly for about a year, and then shifted to semi-monthly (every two weeks) meetings.
- The group stabilized and was comfortable with a membership of eight. We should note here that several pieces of literature suggest a maximum group size of four to six individuals. This usually relates to prayer Ministries that evolve into intimate settings where sensitive personal information is surrendered by those who wish the prayers of the group. Thus, the idea is that with fewer members and stronger mutual support, such sensitive information will be held in stricter confidence.
- The first meetings were centered around a prayer retreat or prayer class.
- AT EVERY MEETING, time is reserved for small group prayer.

Children and Prayer
Children are regularly instructed in prayer life within the parish, usually with members of the prayer Ministry conducting the instruction or helping to "set the stage" for better understanding by the children.

Vestry Prayer Needs
Members of the ministry called members of the Vestry and such groups as the Altar Guild, the Men's Society, etc. on a monthly basis, and asked for their prayer needs. The needs were then screened for any restrictive intimacy and then re-distributed in toto to all those contacted. The prayer

needs were incorporated in the prayer Ministry group as well. Finally, *prayers of thanksgiving* were solicited in response to the answers to previous prayer needs.

This activity serves several purposes beyond the crucial one of the Ministry in petitions/intercession to Jesus Christ on behalf of yourself and others. It brings God's power and wisdom to the activities of the congregation. It keeps the lay leadership aware of the prayer ministry, and of the importance of prayer. It allows you to remind the leadership of the results of prayer. Most important, it encourages the leadership to pray for their activities, and for the activities of others.

Every Member Prayer

An early activity was to insure that all members were lifted to the Lord in prayer on a regular basis. This activity has a group of people, who agree to pray for one person each day, and send that person a not telling them that they have been in the Ministry's prayers.

This activity brings immediate benefits and blessings to those for whom prayers are offered, it brings greater joy and blessing to those who offer the prayers, and it serves to bring the congregation closer together.

Prayer Bulletin

A weekly bulletin insert created as a separate page folded to create a four page bulletin. The back page contains devotional materials related to prayer. The inside section is the weekly prayer requests from the Diocesan list and other listings. The front page list special prayers for missionaries, and for the congregation.

Prayer Care

This program is designed to encourage the congregation in intercessory prayer. A sheet is prepared with the prayer need of one person. Other individuals are included on additional sheets. At the end of Sunday services, the sheets are passed out by the ushers to whomever desires to take one.

The person who takes the sheet agrees to pray for that person during the week, and to fold the sheet into quarters making a small greeting card. The card is sent with a note of encouragement to the person listed.

Prayer Training
Proper training consists of a retreat of one and one-half days of classes in an intensive workshop format. Adult Education includes a multi-week study on prayer. Inquirers classes include an intensive session(s) on prayer. Children's Bible Study includes regular sessions on prayer throughout the year.

Prayer Line
This is a traditional calling tree of people who agreed to receive intercessory prayer needs. The Prayer Line phone number and Email can be published in the phone book and yellow page ad. Non-member prayer line calls have follow-up as a care Ministry and as evangelical outreach.

Appendix Three
Prayer Ministry: A Prayer Retreat

What is a retreat? If you're going full speed ahead right now, the last thing you may have in mind is to retreat. But think about it anyway. **No one can go full speed all the time.** It wears you out. Often the best way to win a war is to stop and retreat. Just rushing ahead can be dangerous. Sometimes you have to stop and get your bearings.

That's a retreat; a time to stop and rest so you can go on again. A time to return to basics: basic attitudes, basic beliefs, the basic balance of life. Above all, a retreat is a rest in God, in whom "we live and move and have our being." "Be still and know that I am God!" (Psalm 40,10) A retreat means, not only to be physically quiet (we're so deluged by noise!), but also to put aside cares and preoccupations.

It is easy to become immersed in the many small details of daily life. It is like hiking in a forest and getting lost because you can't see over the trees. A retreat is like climbing the highest tree in the forest to see clearly the direction one should go. By breaking out of the daily routine by a retreat a person in enabled to put direction back into his life or correct a wandering course.

The prayerful atmosphere and reflection of retreats also helps one to rise above oneself to God. We are social beings. Just like crackers that won't float long in soup without soaking up some of the liquid, so we do the same with the social atmosphere with which we are surrounded. The new and prayerful surroundings of a retreat bring us into a more direct contact with the Divine.

Our Lord went off many times to a desolate place to pray. After one of the apostle's missions of preaching Jesus told them to go off with Him to a desolate place to rest for a while. So both Our Lord and the apostles retreated from the crowds to rest with the Father—to spend time in more concentrated and intimate discourse with Him. They simply retreated or drew back as the word usually means. They pulled back not to run away but to recharge their spiritual batteries. There's an old saying that you can't give someone a drink from an empty well. It has to be filled with water. This is another purpose of making a retreat—to fill our souls with God so that we can go back out into our daily lives radiating His love.

Just as we can get lost in the woods we can get lost in our life of prayer. A retreat can break us out of routine praying and teach us new ways to pray. It can deepen the way we are praying already. On directed retreats there is usually some opportunity for spiritual direction from a priest. We can be helped to understand, improve or correct our life of prayer. At times, God willing, individuals on retreats receive inspirations or have special experiences from the Living God. These can be life changing. Of course, all retreats should have a life changing quality—we should be a different person coming out of them.

We can make our own retreat or find a place that gives retreats. But the point I would like to make here is that we need to make retreats—at least once a year. If the Church requires it of your priest and other religious it means it is important. So let's get back on track or stay on track in our spiritual life and life of prayer by making an annual retreat.

"Come aside and rest awhile," Jesus told his disciples. Otherwise you will get too tired and uncertain of your way. So pick a quiet time and place, if you can, and put what you are doing aside for a while. Enter the room of your own heart, and listen.

About the Author

Rev. Dr. David Sokol served both as college faculty and administration in church related institutions of higher education. He presently directs the Faith Based Division of a national consulting firm and serves as a parish priest and as religious director for the Anglican Sodality of the Most Holy Rosary.

Made in United States
Troutdale, OR
01/03/2025

27552979R00141